Were you to see an angel, you would see a beautiful and lovely creature. Make yourselves like angels in beauty and goodness.

—Brigham Young, *Journal of Discourses* 12:201

Laurel Parker

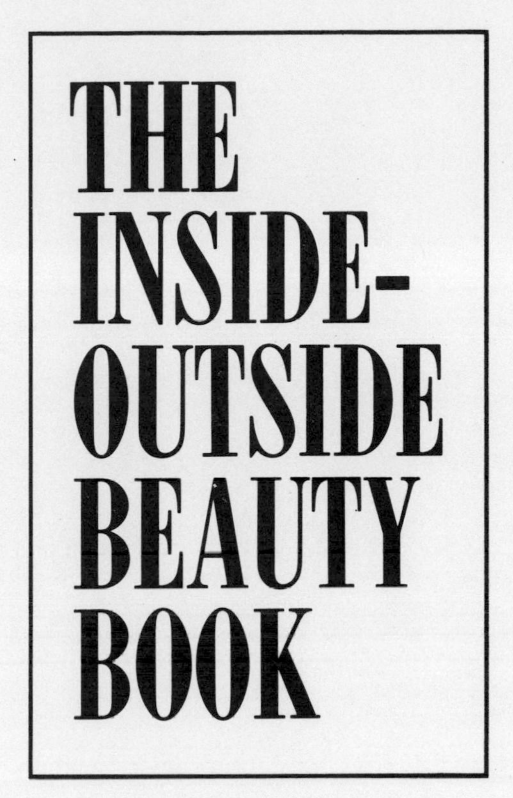


**Barbara Barrington Jones**
**with Sharlene Wells Hawkes**

Deseret Book Company
Salt Lake City, Utah

---

**Library of Congress Cataloging-in-Publication Data**

Jones, Barbara Barrington.
The inside-outside beauty book / by Barbara Barrington Jones.
p. cm.
ISBN 0-87579-271-5
1. Beauty, Personal. I. Title.
RA776.J68 1989
158–dc20 89-37561
CIP

---

Printed in the United States of America

10 9 8 7 6 5 4 3 2 1

*Dedication*

*To the Brigham Young University "Especially for Youth" director, Ron Hills, and his staff and counselors for their enthusiastic, tireless love for the youth of the Church. Proceeds from this book will be used to benefit this wonderful program.*

# CONTENTS

# INTRODUCTION

Imagine that someone has just given you a beautifully wrapped package. The paper is bright and shiny, and the box is circled with wide ribbon, with yards and yards forming the bow. Anything that looks this good just has to have the most incredible gift inside, so you unwrap the present, expecting all kinds of wonderful surprises. Then you open it—and find nothing! The box is empty.

What good does it do to have a beautifully wrapped package when it is nothing but ornamental, nothing but an empty shell?

For years I have worked as an image and fashion consultant, often helping business people and others to develop on the outside a look that accurately reflects what is on the inside: their intelligence, their abilities, and their accomplishments. I also consult with young women who are competing to win beauty titles. In fact, I have been called "the woman behind the beauty queens." I have found that it is useless to help someone become beautiful on the outside if that person does not first have beauty on the inside. The deception will not work. People are quick to uncover that empty kind of beauty. Many of the individuals I have worked with are truly beautiful because they have learned how to balance their lives and have relied on their Heavenly Father to guide them.

My good friend Sharlene Wells Hawkes, a former Miss America, has agreed to participate in this book with me. I am very excited because she is truly an example of someone whose inner commitment to the Lord beautifies her whole life, inside and out. Her advice is invaluable.

In this book, I talk a lot about beauty in a very broad sense. There are some ideas that can help you improve your outside beauty, to give you greater confidence in how you look so you can feel good about yourself. But none of those kinds of improvements really make a difference if you do not make the commitments internally to things of eternal significance, to develop your beauty on the inside.

# ACKNOWLEDGMENTS

Sincere thanks to the following people, without whose help this book would not have been possible:

To my wonderful husband, Hal, who believes in me, loves me, and supports me in everything I do.

To my dear friend Sharlene Wells Hawkes, whose friendship I cherish and who loves and sincerely cares about the young women of the Church.

To Janet Thomas, who took all of my tapes, notes, and videos and compiled them into a manuscript that I could be proud of.

To Eleanor Knowles, who put the finishing touches on my manuscript and saw the book through to publication.

To Richard Erickson and Brent Christison, who designed the book.

To Richard Guy and Rex Holt of Guyrex Associates, friends who have taught me much and who have given me the privilege of helping to train their five Miss USAs.

To Christina Faust, Miss California 1989, and to Laura, Christy, Michelle, Courtney, and Gretchen, those five beautiful Miss USAs, who so graciously helped me in this endeavor.

May God bless each of you.

INNER
BEAUTY

# CHAPTER ONE

## THE GIRL WHO MADE GOOD THINGS HAPPEN

I spend a lot of time speaking to groups of young people about their lives and the things that they want to become. I often receive letters—sad letters, and sometimes letters that scare me. Here is one letter I received:

*Dear Sister Jones,*

*I'm sorry I didn't get to shake your hand, but when I listened to you speak at youth conference, I felt like crying because what you said is what I needed to work on. I really need help!*

*I have always been very shy. I just got my driving permit. I had to take the test twice because the first time I was so scared that I just forgot everything. I have never had very high self-esteem. I am very quiet. I never talk to anyone. I have my patriarchal blessing, but it doesn't sound like it belongs to me the way my life is going. I have always felt like an ugly duckling, I mean really ugly!*

*My father doesn't go to church because he and my mom are divorced, all because he is an alcoholic. I'm 16 and have never gone with anyone. Another one of my problems is that I'm very overweight, and I don't have any self-confidence. I think the Lord has sent you to me and a lot of other girls, but mostly for me. I would like it if you would write me some things that would better my life. Well, I think that's about it for now. I'm really glad I was able to write to you. Thanks for everything,*

*Laurie*

In this book are some of the things that I want Laurie to know.

Let me tell you a story about a girl who, in many ways, started out like Laurie, and what this person did with her life.

There once was a young girl who wore Coke-bottle thick glasses, who was overweight, and whose parents divorced when she was in eighth grade. She went to live with her father and her retarded brother in the country. Suddenly at that young age, she was the acting mother to her little brother, the housekeeper, and the cook on a little ranch where her father trained horses for a living. She had to work very hard, but they were happy for a while. Her father worked six days a week. On Sundays they would all spend the day together. Her father would prepare breakfast, and they would play games, watch football on TV, and eat junk food and pizza. It was their family day.

As this girl got older, one thing made her life very difficult. Her father was very strict. He never let her go on a date, talk on the telephone with friends, or have anyone over to visit. During her junior year of high school, her father came home one afternoon and found that a boy from school had come over to see his daughter. He flew into a rage and started beating her. It was the worst day of her life.

She and her brother were taken out of the custody of her father and sent back to live with her mother. It was during this time, when her life was in an uproar, that, with the support of her mother and her new stepfather, she developed a motto she still lives by: Keep believing in yourself, keep trying, and keep trusting in God. Even though bad things had happened to the girl, her mother kept telling her that God had a plan for her life.

With her mother's help, she started race walking, which helped her to lose weight. During her senior year of high school, she thought she would like to enter the competition for the title of Miss California USA. That was one way she might be able to earn scholarship money for college. She prepared for one solid year. At the pageant, she was selected as first runner-up. Her rising self-esteem took a little dip.

Relying on the assurance that God had a plan for her life, she entered again. She had a strong feeling that participating in the Miss California pageant had something to do with God's plan for her life. This time she was selected as second runner-up.

Most of us would have been devastated, but she did not stop believing in herself. She said, "When they announced my name as second runner-up, I smiled and thought, *It doesn't matter. I'm coming back next year.*"

She got her portfolio together, and through persistence and thorough preparation, she convinced a sponsor to help her in her third bid for Miss California. This time Christina Faust was selected as Miss California USA.

But that's not the end of her story. As Miss California she came to my house for a couple of days in preparation for the Miss USA pageant. In the beginning, I did not know of her great faith. After I had chaperoned her at a benefit appearance for missing children, we started talking. She told me all about her life and then started asking about mine. I told her that my son had just returned from a mission to Argentina.

Christina asked, "Are you Mormons? I've had so many Mormon friends. I just love being around them and their families."

As we were driving into the driveway, I mentioned that I had been a Catholic for thirty-eight years before my family and I joined the Church.

Christina stared at me and said, "You mean Catholics can become Mormons? I want to become a Mormon."

I couldn't believe what I was hearing. All I could say

Christina Faust at age fourteen (above) and as Miss California 1989

was, "You do?" At the same time I was thinking desperately, *Now what do I do? No one is going to believe this.*

The next few days were hectic. With Christina's permission, I invited the missionaries over for dinner, and they started teaching her. She was soaking the missionary lessons up. She was interested in everything. She delayed her departure so she could continue being taught.

The mission president was worried, and I was worried that this was all moving too fast. But Christina reassured me, saying, "God has a plan for my life, and this is part of the plan."

Christina was interviewed by the mission president for baptism, and he later told me he was really touched by her sweet, strong testimony.

The morning of the day she was to be baptized, Christina had an appointment to have her picture taken by a fashion photographer. I went with her. She was posing and smiling, but she kept sneaking looks at her watch. Finally, the photographer asked her why she seemed to be in such a hurry. She said, "Because I don't want to be late for my baptism." Here she was, being fussed over by makeup artists and posing for fabulous pictures, but all she could think about was her baptism. She was not late, and she was baptized that evening.

Shortly after Christina left for the Miss USA pageant, she called me and said, "Barbara, I've been too nervous on stage. I need something to think about. You remember when I went to church with your family, and they had that special program for the Young Women?"

The Young Women in our ward had participated in a sacrament meeting honoring those who had earned their Young Womanhood Recognition. The Young Women theme had been printed on the front of the program.

Christina said, "You remember what was printed on the front of the program? I'm going to memorize that and then repeat it in my mind while I'm standing on stage."

As Christina stood on the stage that evening, she looked radiant—and I knew the reason. She was up there saying in her mind, "I am a daughter of my Heavenly Father who loves me, and I love Him. I will stand as a witness of God at all times . . ."

Her Heavenly Father did indeed have a plan for Christina Faust, and she found out what it was by following her motto: keep believing, keeping trying, and keep trusting in God. Her outer beauty is merely a reflection of what she is on the inside.

Heavenly Father has a plan for each of us that will make us happy. Your plan may not include participating in a beauty pageant as Christina's did, but you can discover the right path. Listen to the best part of yourself, and stay close to your Heavenly Father, and He will guide you.

## The Winning Formula

As I have worked with young women who compete in beauty pageants, I have used what I call my winning formula to help them do as well as they can and to reach their goals. It is a formula that each of us can use in achieving many kinds of goals and in helping us to win many of the battles we face in life.

Anxious to know my secret formula, young women will come to me and ask me to share it. I'll ask them, "If I tell it to you, will you follow it?"

What do you imagine they say? Of course, they say yes.

At that point I could probably tell them anything. If I were to tell them to eat powdered geraniums every day at three o'clock, would they do it? Yes, they would.

But that's not my winning formula. In fact, it is quite a shock to them when we start talking about becoming winners. They may start out thinking I have some secret way to put on makeup, or a trick for selecting the right dress to wear. But those things aren't really important. The things that change a person from head to toe, the things that make her interesting and fun to be around, the things that make her really beautiful are deep inside.

Let me explain what I mean by my winner's formula. It doesn't just have to do with winning beauty pageants; it can change your life, how you look, and how you feel about yourself.

Let's begin with the diagram on page 9.

The outer circle represents *self-discipline.* That is the hardest part, yet it is the vital ingredient that makes the formula work. That is why it encircles everything. Self-discipline is a matter of developing good habits, one day at a time. Developing a habit is like weaving strands. One strand is easy to break, but as you add to that first strand, the strand as a whole becomes increasingly stronger and harder to break. Soon it can develop into a rope that is nearly impossible to break. As you work at developing a habit, each day it will become stronger and more difficult to break. Self-discipline, then, means building rope-strong habits.

Now look at the triangle inside the circle on the diagram.

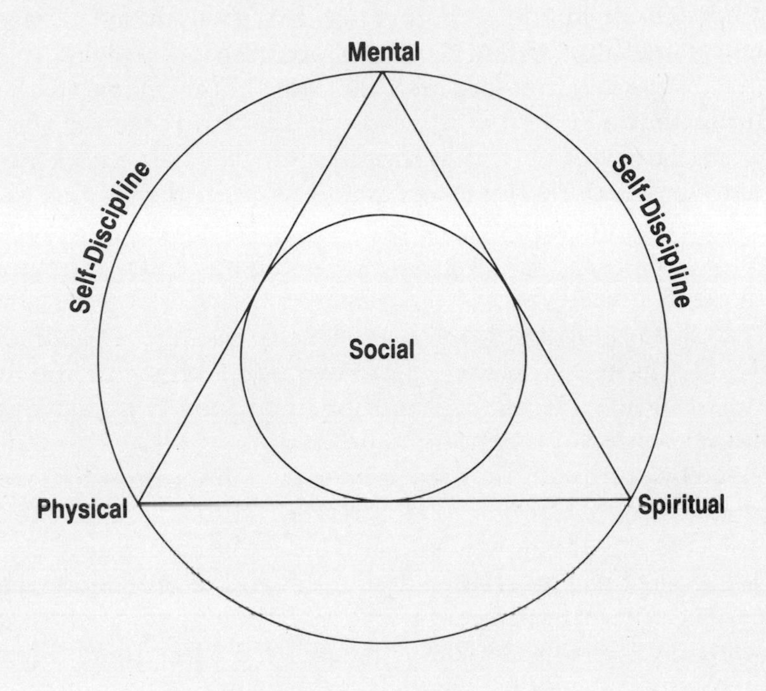


The points of the triangle direct us to three areas of life in which we should discipline ourselves:

1. *Mental.* Improving ourselves mentally means paying attention to the things around us, and taking advantage of opportunities to learn. That doesn't mean taking the easy way out. For example, in school we need to study the basic subjects (yes, that means math, science, English, and history). Those courses may be difficult, but they can also do us a lot of good.

I like this definition of luck: *Luck is when preparation crosses opportunity.* We need to prepare for every opportunity by doing the most that we can, not the least. Learning is a continual process in life; it doesn't end with formal schooling. We all need to keep up on current events by watching the news on television, reading a daily newspaper or weekly newsmagazine, and looking for other ways to improve and stimulate our minds. A bonus to this is that we will always have something to talk to people about.

2. *Physical.* You probably already know many of the things that will help you feel healthier and more fit, such as a balanced diet and sufficient exercise. It is important that we discipline ourselves to follow a good diet and exercise program regularly. You can even combine your physical and mental growth goals by exercising while watching the news on television.

3. *Spiritual.* Disciplining ourselves spiritually has a direct bearing on every facet of life. If we don't keep the line of communication to our Heavenly Father open, we miss our biggest source of inspiration and help.

To be spiritually self-disciplined, it is important to lay a groundwork of prayer and scripture study. Then when problems arise, you can turn to Heavenly Father and say, "It's me again. I just talked to you this morning when I was reading my scriptures and praying. Now I've done all that I can. I have to trust you." If you keep the lines to Him open, you can rely on His help in your life.

Returning to the diagram, the circle inside the triangle represents the social aspects of life. This involves more than just getting to know people. It means extending yourself to make every person you meet feel like a winner. It means being sincere in the compliments you pay people. Every person you come in contact with should feel better for having talked with you that day.

My mother was an excellent example of this. Once when she and I went to a restaurant, our waitress was particularly pleasant. My mother complimented her, as she always does, and then asked her name. The woman told her, and Mother wrote it down on a piece of paper in her purse.

That afternoon Mother went home and got out one of those blank award certificates that you can buy at a stationery store. She wrote on it, "To ____________ (the woman's name), the most outstanding waitress in El Paso,

Texas." Then she sent it to the waitress in care of the restaurant.

The next time I visited my mother, we went to that same restaurant. In a prominent place in the restaurant, we saw that award in a frame on the wall. The waitress had been thrilled to receive it, and her boss had had it framed for display.

This was such a simple thing for my mother to do, yet it was meaningful for a woman who was doing a good job and probably didn't get much recognition for her accomplishments. Mother did things like this all her life. Her thoughtfulness made a difference in many lives.

Each of us can each do similar things in our own way. For example, every time I see one particular bag boy at the grocery store where I shop, I say something like, "You are looking awesome. I mean, every time I come in here you look a little bit more rad." He smiles and blushes about eight shades of red. All I have to do is go a little out of my way to make him feel good about himself.

Another wonderful example of this kind of caring is Courtney Gibbs, Miss USA 1988. One day a twelve-year-old girl with braces asked for her autograph. The girl held her head down so that her braces wouldn't show. Courtney touched the girl's chin and raised her face so they were looking eye to eye. Then she asked, "How long have you had your braces?" Before the girl could answer, Courtney said, "I wore mine for *five years*." The girl burst into a wide grin and said, "I get mine off in six months."

In that moment of sincere caring, Courtney helped that girl feel better about herself. We can show the same kind of concern and caring with others, and it will make a difference in their lives and in ours. If we can make everybody around us feel like a winner, we will feel like winners too.

One great example of someone who followed the winning formula is the Savior. In Luke 2:52 we read, "And Jesus increased in wisdom and stature, and in favour with God and man."

Let me rephrase this scripture a little, adding the words represented in our diagram: "And Jesus increased in wisdom [mental] and stature [physical], and in favour with God [spiritual] and man [social]."

This winning formula really works. It is not a secret restricted to a few individuals—everyone can use it. And it will help you progress in whatever you choose to do.

CHAPTER TWO

# BELIEVE IN YOURSELF

In sixth grade, I was the same height as I am now, which is about five feet ten inches. I wore a size 10AA shoe. I was the one to whom the teacher would say, "Barbara, would you please clean the tops of the blackboards?" When I walked down the hall, I'd miss what was going on because I had to concentrate on getting my arms and legs going the same direction.

My best friend from the sixth grade on was my same height and had the same shoe size as I. Our friends called us the Bobbsey twins. We were both flat chested and had big feet and no waistline. My mother would say, "Barbara, you have a figure just like a sausage." My girlfriend would say, "If one more of those little boys comes up to me and says, 'How's the weather up there?' I'm going to tell him it's raining and then I'll spit right on top of his head."

When we started high school, we thought things would change—maybe the boys would be taller. But it turned out they hadn't grown at all.

In high school there was nothing my friend and I wanted more than to be like the head cheerleader. You know the type. She had long blonde hair and was always tossing her head so that her hair would swing away from her face. She was short, with a great figure, tiny waist, and small feet.

All the guys were always congregating around her locker. We hated it because this girl was so gorgeous and so popular.

One day—I remember it as if it were yesterday—we were walking down this big, long hallway at school, and for once things were different. Here came a gorgeous guy, leather jacket and all. And he was walking toward me. I said to myself, "He's walking toward *moi*." (I was taking French at the time.) I was trying very hard to be cool. When he reached me, he looked me over, then looked down at my shoes and said, "Hey, hon, do those come equipped with oars?"

Can you imagine how I felt then? I went home that afternoon and threw myself across my bed and cried my eyes out. I hated being tall. All I ever wanted was to be short.

In high school I had only two really significant dates. One was to the senior prom. I borrowed a dress from a girl who was bigger on top than I was and stuffed the bodice of the dress with several scarves. The big evening came. My date came to pick me up, and as I got into his car, he looked over and saw a little tip of red at the top of my bodice. "What's this?" he asked. Before I could stop him, he started pulling—and pulled a whole red scarf out of the top of my dress. And then he started snickering. I was devastated!

When I look back at my high school years now, I realize that I wasted too much time wishing I could be like someone else and thinking poorly of myself. But I really wasn't anywhere close to being a failure. I was an honor student. I did well in tough classes. I was also a classical ballet dancer—I had studied dancing from the time I was six years old. I had many strengths, but I couldn't see them. I spent my time wishing I could change things that were not possible to change. I wished I were shorter, but there wasn't a thing I could do about it. I couldn't go on a diet and lose three inches.

I also don't know what the head cheerleader wished she could change, but I can guarantee that she wished something were different in her life. Maybe she wished that she were taller.

It took me years to realize that every girl compares herself to others. The letters I receive and the comments I hear from girls all over the country have convinced me of that. The challenge is to learn to recognize our strengths and to make the most of them, not to dwell on our weaknesses or the things we cannot change. One girl who learned the importance of recognizing your own strengths wrote to me:

*I'm not very good in school. I don't play in sports. I tried to play softball once but I was awful. I danced for a year, and I was actually all right. At least that's what my teacher said. But I felt so stupid. I was the only fourteen-year-old in the class, and everyone else was seven or eight. You know how stupid I felt. My last two boyfriends broke up with me because they didn't want their friends thinking they were going out with such an ugly girl.*

*Recently I filled out the forms for the Miss Teen USA pageant because you and my mother are the only ones in my life who ever told me I was pretty. When my mom said I was pretty, it was kind of like she had to say it because she's my mom. But it's nice to hear someone else say it. That's why I wrote: to tell you thank you.*

*Love, Jenny Bucheit*

Jenny competed in the Miss Teen USA pageant for California. She never dreamed she would be competing on stage in a state beauty pageant, but she did. Her friends couldn't see the outstanding, beautiful girl she is because she had them talked into seeing her as she saw herself, as an ugly girl. She found that if you tear yourself down all the time, others will believe you.

Another young woman who taught me a great deal about how important it is to be your own person was Michelle Royer, Miss USA 1987. Two weeks before she won

Jenny Bucheit, whose goal was to compete for Miss Teen USA from California

the national title, Michelle won an important victory: she found out that she didn't have to be a carbon copy of anybody else. She could be herself, and that was a very good person to be. Here is the letter she wrote to the directors of the Miss Texas pageant:

*I could never really put into words how much I appreciate you or how much I've grown in the past few months. When people ask me how you have helped me, I tell them that besides giving me Texas on a silver platter, you have given me the opportunity to learn on my own. Never before have I been able to rely so much on myself; that is a pretty good feeling, considering the next month ahead of me. It sure feels good not to be scared anymore. Some of my so-called friends in school and other beauty pageants that I've been in made me—or should I say I let them make me—feel insecure because I never could fit into a mold. You taught me that there is no mold for Michelle Royer. I'm the only person like me, thank goodness.*

Michelle Royer,
Miss USA 1987,
who tells young women,
"When God made you,
He broke the mold.
You are uniquely special."

*I hope that you will be as proud of me on February 17, when I compete in the Miss USA pageant, as I am to be Miss Texas. Thanks for everything.*

*Love always,*
*Michelle Royer*

We were very proud of her. She won the Miss USA crown, but she had already won a great victory before the pageant finals.

My point is that we never seem to see ourselves correctly. The day we do see clearly is the day we become free—free to be our own best selves. That person, our true self, is the one that others will find attractive and fun to be with.

## THE REAL YOU

It is easy to compare ourselves to others and come up short. Why don't I have the talent that she does? Why can't I play the piano like she does? Why can't I sing? But I believe that Heavenly Father gave everyone special talents. We just have to each find our own particular talents and make the most of them—to accept what we can't change, improve what we can improve, and know that we are all winners.

Many people seem to believe that acting like someone or something they are not is better than being who they really are deep down inside. Having worked with many beauty queens in a business that is often accused of being superficial, I have seen some delightful examples of young women who have learned who they really are, and who are loved and admired because they have been true to themselves.

Young women preparing for beauty pageants often make the mistake of telling judges what they think those judges want to hear. They come off sounding like this: "If I win Miss America, I want to go to Ethiopia and feed all the starving children, and I'm going to plant seeds and kiss everyone I meet along the way."

A couple of years ago, I asked one contestant, "If you won ten thousand dollars, what would you do with it?" She fell into the trap of answering how she thought I would want her to answer. She said, "Well, I'd probably give it all to the American Cancer Society."

I confronted her and said, "Come on! If you won that money, you know you'd probably go out and buy yourself a new wardrobe or car or something exciting like that."

Although we don't have to face interviews with a panel of judges very often in our lives, we are still tempted to put up a false front that seems preferable to our real selves. I tell the young women I work with, "Just relax and be the real you, the one that shows up when you are sitting at your kitchen table. The real you is the best you."

Laura Martinez-Herring, Miss USA 1985, says: "People will love being around you if you are happy, positive, and enthusiastic. The real you is the best you."

One person who learned to be her own best self was Laura Martinez-Herring of Texas. She was a determined young woman who wanted desperately to be the stereotypical beauty queen, soft spoken and a stately five feet nine with a willowy figure.

But Laura wasn't like that. She was five feet six and a little bit overweight, to begin with. However, she was also a dynamic, vivacious person, one could wear dangling earrings and a big ponytail, tied with a yellow scarf, on the side of her head. She had tremendous enthusiasm and a positive attitude.

Laura was born in Los Mochis, Sinaloa, Mexico. She earned enough money to spend her senior year of high school in Switzerland, where she studied French. Then she and her sister took their backpacks and toured the world. In India she joined a volunteer organization and found herself hoeing fields and cleaning toilets. She had never worn makeup or a pair of high heels when she walked into pageant offices in El Paso and announced, "I'm the next Miss USA." The officials there laughed at first, but little by little, Laura started fixing herself up, and eventually she won the Miss El Paso title and went onto the Miss Texas pageant.

The night she became Miss Texas, Laura approached the table where I was sitting at the coronation ball, crouched down next to my chair, and said, "I know I don't know you, but I know you're going to help me. I'll do anything you say. I don't care what it takes." I have never seen anybody in my life as positive or determined as she was. I told her later, as she worked with me in my home, "Laura, be the real you. That's how you will win."

When a young woman goes into an interview with the judges, it is important that she have a story to tell. Laura was told, "No matter what the judges ask you, find a way to tell them that you cleaned toilets in India. That will get their attention, and they'll never forget you." It was our private joke that when she walked into her interview with the judges, she would say, "Speaking of toilets . . . "—and then she would tell her story.

Laura captured the judges' attention and was crowned Miss USA 1985. She found her own best assets—her tremendous enthusiasm and positive attitude—and she let those things shine through. And people loved and admired her because she let her true self show.

It is a mistake for any of us to think that we can run away from our responsibilities and find ourselves. We can't say, "Well, if I go traveling all over the world, maybe I'll find who I really am." It doesn't work like that. Each of us must turn to another source to find our true self. We are all children of our Heavenly Father. That is our divine nature. He is our Father. And because of that divine relationship, we can have confidence that our true selves are worthwhile.

A friend of my husband, Hal, told us a story one day about his little granddaughter. At Christmastime the girl and her grandfather were walking past a store window, and they stopped to look at a display of Santa Claus dolls from various countries. One was most unusual, dressed in a beautiful white velvet robe with gold trim. Since the doll was not wearing the usual red costume trimmed with white, the grandfather asked, "Do you know who that is?" She looked at the doll and said, "Yes, Grandpa. That's my Heavenly Father." Then with tears in her eyes, she added, "I miss him so much."

To get to know who you really are, it is important to keep the lines of communication open with Heavenly Father. This might be likened to walking into a room when the light isn't on. You can look at the ceiling and see the light bulb there, and you know that all you have to do to get light is flip a switch. The light bulb is connected to wires that go through the walls of the house, down the block, and eventually to the source of the power. But the switch doesn't turn itself on. You have to flip the switch.

The same principle might be applied to communicating with God. He's always there, waiting for you to come and talk, any time, any place, for any amount of time. But you have to "flip the switch" to start the communication. It is important to do this often and regularly. Then when the really big problems come, you will recognize that still, small voice that brings His messages to you.

CHAPTER THREE

# EIGHT SOURCES OF SELF-ESTEEM

We often hear people blame their problems on a lack of self-esteem. But if a person doesn't have much self-esteem, how does she go about getting more? Sometimes it seems like an impossible situation.

Before we talk about how to improve self-esteem, try this little exercise. Take a piece of paper and write down your answers to this question: "If someone had a magic wand and could give me the desires of my heart, what would they be?"

Write down the things that will make *you* feel better about *yourself,* not things you wish other people would do. Now, read on. We'll come back to your answers later.

Most of the time people wait for others to tell them how they should feel and how they should act. They wait for someone else to tell them that they are doing a good job before they believe that they really are doing well. This is a natural response: We all need to know that others admire us and like us. The problem comes when we stop listening to ourselves and believe only outside voices.

I have two friends, one a nun and the other a producer in Hollywood, both of whom are single, and each of whom has discovered a great secret. They agree that if you can't find peace within yourself, no outside circumstances will ever help you.

Recently I counseled with a young woman who had bulimia. She told me how one day she had sat in her room and eaten one hundred laxatives. She said she couldn't go to church on Sunday mornings because she threw up quite often. She had lost her job, and she had lost a wonderful man whom she liked very much. "He's wonderful," she said, "everything I ever wanted in a husband. Why did he dump me?"

I answered by asking her a question: "How would you feel if a young man came to you and said, 'I'm madly in love with you, but I have this problem. I take one hundred laxatives a day. I throw up. I lost my job. I know I'm obese. I hate myself.' "

Then she knew what had happened. Her ex-boyfriend was looking for a woman who was happy with herself, and she wasn't. We have to learn to be happy with ourselves. We can't look to others to give us our sense of self-worth. It is something we must do for ourselves.

Remember, self-esteem is not a constant thing throughout your life. It's like a roller coaster. There will always be ups and downs. That's normal. Just when you think things are going well and should keep going up forever, suddenly you'll have a setback. At different times in everyone's life, there will be periods of low self-esteem. You just have to hang in there and keep trying, and your self-esteem will start rising again.

How does a person develop self-esteem? If this is a problem for you, here are eight important factors that can affect how you feel about yourself:

1. *Peer Pressure*

How much are your feelings about yourself based on what others say about you—or what you perceive they think about you?

When you receive a compliment, how do you react? Suppose someone says, "Your hair looks great today." Do you respond, "Oh, my hair has never looked so bad – I can't do a thing with it"? If someone says, "You're such a wonderful pianist," do you answer, "Oh, today it was okay, but I don't really play that well"?

When you respond to compliments in a negative or self-deprecating way, your self-esteem apparently depends not on what is said to you, but on how you perceive it. If you think that people have ulterior motives or if in your response to them you belittle yourself, then your self-esteem is low. On the other hand, if someone says, "Your hair looks great" and you respond with a simple "Thank you," your self-esteem is high.

2. *Personal Performance and Expectations*

How much does your performance in work, school, or other activities affect your self-esteem? It is not actually what you do, but how you feel about what you do that makes a difference. You might be concerned about your grades; an athlete might be concerned about an important race or game; a beauty queen might worry how well she performs on stage and in interviews. Can you feel comfortable with doing your best even if others achieve greater recognition or higher standing, or must you always win?

Let's say you are usually a very orderly and organized person. But you've had a very busy day. Unexpected things came up, so you didn't make your bed, and your room is a mess. In English class your teacher sprang a surprise quiz. You offered to help with decorations for the school prom, and they have to be picked up today, but your dad needs the car. An article you agreed to write for the school paper is due tomorrow, but you haven't had time yet to interview the people involved. Your neighbors call and are desperately looking for someone to babysit while they visit a sick relative in the hospital. You've had a whole day of this, and you're exhausted. Then your mother comes in and makes some kind of remark like, "Looks like you didn't get much done today, did you!"

If your self-esteem is high, you can remain calm and

say, "This day was just hard. I did the very best I could, and I feel good about it."

If your self-esteem is low, you may allow your mother's comment to make you feel worthless. All of a sudden you start doubting yourself and wondering if you actually are doing things well.

Remember, everybody expects perfection. Parents expect perfection in their children—and children expect perfection in their parents. Actually, this is unfair. None of us is perfect; we are all trying to do the best we can with our own circumstances, and it isn't fair to judge others or to let others' reactions to us affect how we feel about ourselves.

3. *Expressing Your Feelings*

Can you show your true feelings?

If you are angry, can you tell someone how you feel? If your self-esteem is high, you should be able to express your feelings. You can talk to others and trust that they will not be judgmental. You can say, "I'm really angry about this. I hope you will listen to me." But if you are the type of person who holds all that in and hides your feelings, your self-esteem needs to be built up.

Experts in counseling believe that we need to share our frustrations. Try talking to your parents. If you can't talk comfortably with them, then think of other trusted adults or friends with whom you can share your problems and frustrations. At the core of anger is hurt or frustration. Being able to share your feelings can help foster better self-esteem.

4. *Acknowledging Your Imperfections*

Can you let people know what is really inside of you? Can you trust people enough to let them in, to let them know your weaknesses?

For example, I see the new Relief Society president coming up my driveway, and I am a wreck. I still have my jogging suit on and it's noon. I haven't put my makeup on. The dishes are piled high in the sink. My hair is in rollers. Can I open the door?

This really happened to me one day. Here I was, the

lady who works with beauty queens, looking like a mess but wanting to make a good impression on the new Relief Society president. I waited until she got to the porch. Then I swung open the door and sang, "Here I am, Miss America." She burst out laughing.

I invited her in and said, "Well, this is the real me." By admitting that I had weaknesses, I gave the message that my self-esteem—at least in that area—was high. If it had been low, I would have hidden and not answered the door. I would have avoided letting anyone know about my weaknesses.

The nice thing about admitting your weaknesses is that in doing so, you communicate to others that you are human. People usually like us better when they know that we aren't perfect.

5. *Real versus Ideal*

How do you see yourself with respect to how you think you should be? We're not talking here about the "ideal you" from your parents' point of view. It's your ideal self. Imagine a self-esteem scale of one to ten, with ten being the very top, your "perfect self." At the bottom of the scale, with a score of one, is complete lack of self-esteem, a self who is full of imperfections and weaknesses. Where would you place yourself on this scale? Are you a three? a five? an eight?

Most people I meet will put themselves at three or four—or, at the most, five.

Those whose self-esteem is high usually feel good about themselves most of the time. They bounce back when negative things happen. Those who have low self-esteem say there isn't much use in trying. They feel uncomfortable when they receive compliments. They believe that they have little control over their future, and even that things will get worse in the future. They believe that they are being controlled by external situations. They often feel depressed and at fault when something goes wrong.

Remember, no matter how you feel about yourself today, your self-confidence is like the roller coaster. At certain times in your life, your self-esteem can be high—and then suddenly it can plummet. But one thing is certain in life: that things will change. Knowing that things can change and will get better can help us through those low times when we feel discouraged and depressed.

6. *Physical Well-Being*

Do you have a general sense of feeling good and alive and at ease with yourself? At a Miss Universe pageant I was once introduced at a board of directors meeting as "the body lady." In a way, that fits, because I truly believe that a person's physical well-being affects how that person feels and acts. I believe that what we eat and how we exercise play a major role in how we feel about ourselves.

If you have energy, that feeling of being alive and eager to face each day and each new situation, you will have higher self-esteem. If you feel depressed, don't seem to have any energy, and don't sleep well or have difficulty getting up in the morning, you will have lower self-esteem.

I have an aunt who had trouble getting along with her new husband's teenage daughter. They crossed swords constantly. The strain made my aunt absolutely miserable. I advised her, "Go take an aerobics class. Get out and do something. Don't just dwell on this one problem."

She joined a group of women who took an exercise class together, and she found that she really enjoyed the physical exercise. She later told me, "Barbara, when I get home now and my stepdaughter is yelling and carrying on, I refuse to fight back anymore or let it affect how I feel. Exercise has helped me be much calmer and feel much better about myself."

If you want your physical self-esteem to be high, then you have to work on it. You have to get enough sleep. You have to exercise. You have to eat right. You can't just take the easy way out and say, "But I don't have time to do that." You don't have time *not* to do those things that will improve your health—and your self-esteem.

7. *Comparing Yourself with Others*

Do you frequently compare yourself with others? If your self-esteem is high, you will tell yourself, "I wouldn't trade with anyone." If your self-esteem is low, you will find yourself saying, "I wish I were as thin as so-and-so," or "I wish I had a personality like her."

During the Miss USA pageant in 1986, Christy Fichtner, Miss Texas, called me on the phone and lamented, "Barbara, I'm not as pretty as Miss New York. I don't have as nice a wardrobe as Miss California. I don't have as sparkling a personality as Miss Nevada." She went through every state in the Union! By comparing herself to others, she nearly destroyed her self-confidence and all that she had worked for. She couldn't eat and wasn't sleeping well, all because she could see only the good points everyone else had that she seemed to lack.

I managed to reassure Christy that she really was a winner and had as good a chance to win the title as any other competitor. Later, after she had won the title, she was at my house counseling a young lady I was working with. She said, "One of the worst things we can do is to compare ourselves with others."

All of us occasionally get caught in the self-comparison trap. A while ago at a youth conference, I observed a well-known youth speaker who, as he gave his talk, told jokes and had all the youths laughing with him. That evening I watched him as he walked into the dance. He reached out, grabbed a young man by the shoulder, and asked, "What's your name?"

The young man replied, "Chris."

Then this popular speaker said, "Chris, I love you."

As I watched this scene, I was embarrassed for my fellow speaker. I thought, *What is that young man thinking right now? I could never walk up to a stranger like that and say, "What's your name?" and "I love you." That's just not me.*

In a testimony meeting at the end of the conference, Chris stood up and said, "You know, when I walked into that dance, a man that I had never met before walked up to me and asked my name. Then he said he loved me. I thought to myself, I haven't been living righteously. I don't deserve somebody's love. But this guy said he loved me. I knew he meant it. This whole conference, I've been thinking about it. And I've decided that if someone could love me and not even know me, I'm just going to change my life."

Listening to this young man bear his testimony brought tears to my eyes. I wanted to have that kind of influence on young people.

In this life we each have to use and magnify our own talents. Heavenly Father has given each individual many talents, and it doesn't do any good to compare ourselves to others and wish we had their particular strengths and talents. All that does is lower our own self-esteem.

8. *Physical Appearance*

When you look in the mirror, do you like what you see? Feeling good about yourself and how you look is critical to your self-esteem. If you feel negative about what you see, then there are some things you can probably do to change your image. But remember, dieting won't make you three inches shorter, if you feel you're too tall. Some physical attributes are hereditary, such as your height, the color of your eyes, and your general body build. There are some things you'll just have to accept about your physical appearance.

However, there are things you can do with your dress and makeup that can help you feel better about yourself. Each person has attributes that make that person unique. That is why it is important to learn who *you* are and what you can do to enhance *your* image. And paying attention to how you look can affect how others react to you, an important consideration to build your self-esteem.

One woman I know has a unique kind of natural beauty. She doesn't wear any makeup and she doesn't need to. Her face has a beautiful, natural glow. She always looks lovely. And wearing royal blue eye shadow and black eyeliner would not do anything to enhance her appearance—in fact, it would be totally wrong for her.

Sometimes young women will look at others and try to adopt a look that really isn't right for them. Have you ever heard someone say—or have you ever said—"I wish I could be like so-and-so"? Or have you ever become discouraged when you have met someone whom you admire and said to yourself, "I could never be like her"?

You can never be exactly like anyone else, so it's important to find what will make *you* look good and feel comfortable. If you are a sporty and casual type of person, select clothes and makeup that will enhance that image. If you see yourself with a more classic image, select styles that are appropriate to that image.

While it is important to pay attention to your clothes and your grooming, that doesn't mean you have to spend a lot of money doing so. You don't. Attractive and flattering styles and grooming supplies and makeup are available at budget prices. One of the most important things you can do for yourself is to become more aware of your appearance and how it is perceived by others.

Don't be afraid to make changes. Sometimes a change is just what we need to improve our self-esteem. Try a new hairstyle. Experiment with your makeup. At the very least, try a different shampoo or hand lotion. Change means action, and action is often necessary to build self-esteem. Make sure you like yourself, and if you don't, then change. Don't wallow in the comfort of discomfort.

Now, remember the list you made earlier? If you are like the majority of those who have responded when I have asked them to list the desires of their heart, you probably included some of the following wishes. This is the order in which these desires are listed most frequently:

1. Lose weight.
2. Do well at school or at work.
3. Develop greater confidence.

4. Develop a talent.
5. Improve my appearance.
6. Develop a more positive attitude.
7. Become better organized.
8. Develop greater patience and self-control.
9. Have more money.

The bottom line is that if you don't like yourself, you need to find ways to overcome those things you don't like and, in the process, to build your self-esteem. If you do like yourself, you will have greater confidence in your own abilities and talents and your relationships with others will be satisfying. It's up to you!

CHAPTER
FOUR

## APPLYING THE WINNER'S FORMULA

After Laura Martinez-Herring won the title of Miss USA in 1985, I was on stage in the crowd gathered around her when a pretty blonde girl came up to me and tapped me on the shoulder. She introduced herself as Christy Fichtner and said she was going to be competing the next year for the title of Miss Texas. She also said she hoped she would win so she could come and work with me to prepare for the Miss USA pageant.

I thought it was nice that she sought me out, but I didn't really think any more about it. The next time I saw Christy was during the Miss Texas pageant. I was sitting in the lobby of my hotel, and Christy came up to me and said, "Do you remember me? I'm getting ready to compete for the title of Miss Texas. I sure hope I win so I can work with you."

She had changed a great deal even in the few months since I had seen her at the Miss USA pageant. She did beautifully in the Miss Texas competition and won the title, so it was arranged that I would help her prepare for the Miss USA competition.

When I work with young women who are preparing for beauty pageants, I have them come to my home in California for a few days. We practice walking, prepare for the inter-

Christy Fichtner,
Miss USA 1986:
"My advice is that you master the winner's word NO. Listen to the promptings of the Spirit and then follow what you know to be right."

views they will have, and talk about the importance of exercise, good nutrition, and physical appearance. Most important, though, we talk about the importance of their self-image and what they are inside.

For some reason I felt prompted to call our stake president's wife and ask her if we might be able to give a fireside during Christy's stay. Though Christy was not a member of the Church, I felt that she was a lovely role model for the teenagers in our stake. Permission was given, and we began planning the fireside.

That Sunday I was to give the cultural refinement lesson in Relief Society and to speak at the fireside that evening. I asked my husband to give me a blessing to help me with those assignments, and I invited Christy to be present. She listened to the blessing carefully, and then we went to Relief Society. I noticed a few tears during the lesson.

That night Christy was to introduce me at the fireside.

She looked over the assembled group and said, "I have such a warm feeling when I walk into the chapel. You may have heard of a friend of mine, Steve Young [the professional football player]. He and his family introduced me to the Church when I was in high school. The more I see of it, the warmer my feelings are. I guess I'm almost bearing my testimony. I don't know if I have a definite one to give, but this is just the way I feel."

I was flabbergasted. The fireside went well, and as we were getting ready to sing the closing hymn, Christy leaned over to me and said, "Barbara, I want to be baptized." I said, "Christy, I think you'd better go home and pray about this."

When she greeted me the next morning Christy said, "Barbara, I still feel the same."

The next few days were busy. Christy had already learned a lot about the Church in her teens. Now the missionaries formally taught her the lessons. The bishop asked my son, John, who had just received his mission call to Argentina, to baptize her.

Looking back on this experience I wonder, Why did Christy want to be baptized? What made her have those feelings? One day I read Ether 4:11: "But he that believeth these things which I have spoken, him will I visit with the manifestations of my Spirit, and he shall know and bear record. For because of my Spirit he shall know that these things are true; for it persuadeth men to do good."

That was what Christy was feeling. She made her choice, but it wasn't the easiest choice. I know the temptations she had to face in the world as a celebrity. If you drank or smoked, you might fit in with the group. But Christy had mastered the winner's word: No!

Before winning her title, Christy was a model with the Eileen Ford agency, one of the most famous modeling agencies in the world. And she was dating a professional golfer from Spain who had a reputation as a wild, wonderful man. She was supposed to fly to Spain for an assignment, and the golfer arranged to be on the same plane. But before she left, Christy got a call from Eileen Ford. As Christy tells it, Eileen was very blunt. She told Christy, "Don't let him have you. Men like him like the challenge. The more you play the game, the more they'll hang onto you. For them, the challenge is the fun. And when they've had you, the game is over—the fun is over."

Christy had already been making right decisions, and so she said no to this man.

As a beauty pageant winner, Christy has been invited many places, but she has always stuck to her beliefs. Frequently people offer her alcoholic drinks. Once at a party in Hollywood, a movie producer came up to her and handed her a glass of champagne.

Christy said, "No, thank you."

He offered her a cigarette. She said, "No, thank you."

"That was all I had to say," she later told me. "When they were passing around the cocaine at the end of the party, all I had to say was, 'No thank you. It's not my thing.' "

That's how she handles everything. She told me once, "It's so simple, Barbara. If I could be with you as you speak to young women, I would just tell them to say, 'No, thank you.' "

Now, I realize that great pressures can be placed on people as they are faced with choices. But Christy has learned what we all have to learn: to be loyal to herself and what she believes. She has earned the respect of many people because she can say no and stick to it.

The day before Christy Fichtner went out on stage to compete in the 1986 Miss USA pageant in Miami, she was really in distress. She had nearly destroyed her self-confidence by uselessly comparing herself with the other competitors.

I asked her, "Christy, would you like to have a blessing?"

"Oh, yes!" she said.

Through a series of small miracles, I was able to contact

a bishop who worked in a building near our hotel, and he agreed to come give Christy a blessing. He brought with him another member of the Church who was a professor at Miami University. The only private place we could find was virtually a closet.

The two priesthood holders laid their hands on Christy's head and the bishop gave her a blessing. Among other things he said, "Christy, your Heavenly Father is proud of you, and He wants you to know that when you walk out on that stage tonight, He will be there with you."

Tears were streaming down her cheeks when Christy stood and thanked him and then hugged me. I later wrote in my journal what she said after that blessing: "Barbara, it's not my problem anymore. My Heavenly Father is going to be with me."

When she walked out on the stage that evening, Christy was truly beautiful, with that aura of peace that comes only from a heavenly source. She had done everything in her power to that point, and now she trusted that the Lord would decide what was best for her.

Earlier we talked about my winner's formula and the importance of having balance in our lives. Christy had applied that formula by developing herself physically, mentally, spiritually, and socially, and then, when she had done all that she could do, she left the rest to God and trusted Him.

In the Bible we are told: "Delight thyself also in the Lord; and he shall give thee the desires of thine heart. Commit thy way unto the Lord; trust also in him; and he shall bring it to pass." (Psalm 37:4-5.)

This formula can help you in your life. If you do your part diligently and then act according to what you know is right, you can know that He is God and that He will be with you. Trust Him.

CHAPTER FIVE

# NEVER STOP TRYING

I always wanted to be a dancer.

I started taking dancing lessons when I was six. By the time I was twelve, I thought I was getting pretty good. In our school they had a Christmas program, and the physical education teacher was selecting girls to do a modern-dance arrangement of the beautiful carol "O Holy Night." All of the physical education classes learned the dance, and I thought, *I am a ballet dancer, so I'm sure I'm going to be chosen to do "O Holy Night" for the Christmas program.* I learned the dance, and I thought I did it really well. But when the selections were made, I was not chosen. I was crushed. I thought, *Here I have been taking classes for six whole years, and I can't do anything right.*

When I was fourteen, I got my first dance solo. It was in a ballet production of *The Merry Widow.* A male dancer was brought in from Mexico City, and I was selected to dance the "Merry Widow Waltz" with him. I worked really hard at rehearsals. After the first performance, I ran off the stage thinking, *Boy, I'm really in the big time now. I really did a good job.* But my teacher merely looked at me and said in a disgusted voice, "You looked just like a football player." I was crushed again.

Of course, I was practicing and improving all the time.

I did have successes, but I just couldn't see them. I was always judging my dancing by these failures.

At fifteen I was asked to audition for Ballet Russe, which at that time was one of the the most outstanding ballet companies in America. My parents flew me to Houston, where I had a special appointment with the director. I was so scared that I could not do one thing right. I was literally petrified, and I made a fool of myself. Needless to say, I wasn't selected for the Ballet Russe. I went home feeling totally dejected. Though I had been dancing since I was six years old, I felt that I was still awful. However, I kept on dancing, and I did have opportunities to dance with the University Civic Ballet Company.

After graduating from high school, I went to New York City, expecting to take that city by storm. Someone got stormed all right, and it was me. When I looked around at the other dancers in my advanced ballet class, I thought, *nobody in this whole class is worse than I am.* Looking back, I can now see that I was actually pretty good. But back then, I just knew that nobody could possibly be worse than I was.

A few months after I arrived in New York, I auditioned for the Ballet Russe again. I didn't make it. Then I went to a Jerome Robbins audition. About three hundred dancers were there, and I was eliminated in the first group.

That was a difficult year for me. I had left home being the most self-centered person on the face of the earth. I couldn't wait to get away from home. To my dismay my parents had even arranged for me to stay in a convent in New York, so I'd be protected and supervised!

One incident that winter seemed to represent my year. I was taking four ballet classes a day and commuting on the subway. My feet were a mass of blisters. I wear a size ten shoe, and my toe shoes were a size seven and a half. Talk about pain! When my point class ended one afternoon, I knew that with all my blisters I couldn't put on my street shoes, so I asked the girl who had the locker next to mine if I could borrow her shower shoes. They were big and floppy, but I put them on anyway. Then I put on my leg warmers, bundled up in my black wool coat and black bonnet with fake fur trim, and started out in the snow for the subway.

It was rush hour, so the subway was very crowded and I had to stand, holding onto one of the straps hanging from the ceiling. The first stop was Grand Central Station, and hordes of people rushed for the doors to get off while others were pushing their way onto the train. I held on with all my might, but with all the pushing and shoving, the shower shoes came off my feet and were pushed out the door—which shut before I could rescue them. Now I was standing in the subway train barefooted. When I arrived at my stop near the end of the line in the Bronx, I had to walk barefoot, with blistered feet, all the way up the hill to the convent.

My feet freezing, I stumbled home crying all the way. *If only my mother were here,* I thought. *She was so good to me. She always picked me up from ballet. I never had to walk anywhere. She'd have picked me up and brought me home in this horrible storm.* I surely missed my mother.

Then I came down with the flu. My room was freezing most of the time, because a big crack in the window had let the snow in during the night. That morning I woke up with a high fever and feeling terrible. All I could think was, *Where's my mother?* If my mother had been there, all I would have had to say was, "Mother, would you please bring me some soup?" and she would. But now I had no mother or anyone else to take care of me. I can remember getting out of bed, dressing, and then dragging myself out in the snow to the little store on the corner to get some 7-Up because my stomach was so upset. All the way I cried, and all the way I wished my mother were there. I thought of the brat I had been those last years in high school, and I wished she were there now so I could tell her how much I loved her and how much she meant to me.

As I continued to feel sorry for myself, my eating habits changed. I started eating as a way to compensate. On my route to the subway, I passed four bakeries, and every day I would stop and buy sweet rolls. As a result, I started gaining weight.

One afternoon I was called into the office of the ballet school and told that if I didn't lose weight, I would be sent home. I was devastated. I went back to the convent, and in my mailbox was a letter from my father. I was so excited that I couldn't wait to open it. I loved my father very much, but he was a man of few words and didn't write often. But whenever he did write, I paid attention! I opened the envelope (I was eating a powdered doughnut at the time—my fourth one that day) and found a poem he had written, titled "Ode to a 'Budding' Ballerina":

*Donuts, hot dogs, stuff like that*
*Is bound to make a body fat.*
*So if you're going to eat that way,*
*You'll wind up in the blimp ballet.*

*Unless the trend is toward a show*
*Of baby elephants on toe,*
*I would suggest you put the brake*
*Upon your heavy junk intake.*

The next day I went to the ballet school, and I showed them Dad's poem. They posted it on the bulletin board, and I decided to go on a diet. But never having been on a diet in my life, I didn't know where to start. I walked down to the chapel there in the convent and knelt down. Then, for the first time in my life, I really talked to my Father in heaven. I poured out my heart to Him and said, "Please help me. This is the biggest goal I have in my life, to be a ballerina, and I have to lose weight."

I walked out of the chapel just as a woman carrying a suitcase walked in the door looking very lost. I asked if I could help her, and she said she was entering the convent and couldn't find her room. She had a room key in her hand, so I took her to her room and helped her get settled.

As we talked, I asked her what her profession was. She said, "I'm a nurse—but more specifically, I'm a dietitian."

I thought, *God really does hear prayers! He heard mine, and He sent me an angel disguised as a nurse.*

I asked her if she could help me lose weight. She agreed and helped work out a diet plan. I went from 150 pounds to 116. (But it turned out that I had to go home anyway because I was anemic.)

I did have one positive experience before I left New York. My girlfriend talked me into auditioning for the Radio City Music Hall Corps de Ballet. I had done so badly in so many auditions that I didn't really care. But I went with my friend—and I was offered a contract.

On the advice of my ballet teacher, I turned the offer down, but it was very flattering. And I did learn something from that experience. In order to do your best, you have to reach a point where you can really tell yourself that the outcome is not going to make or break your life. Only then can you have true confidence.

After I went home, I entered a local Miss America preliminary in the state of Texas and won based largely on my ballet talent. Again, I felt that if I didn't win, it didn't matter. My life didn't depend on that contest.

I had seven more years of training and struggle before I finally reached my goal of being a professional ballet dancer. I was the ballet mistress of the University Civic Ballet Company. I was a guest choreographer and assistant artistic director for the Corpus Christi Civic Ballet and taught ballet at the University of Texas and in my own studio for a time. It wasn't until I was twenty-six that I signed my first professional contract with the Atlanta Ballet Company.

As I look back on these experiences, I recognize that the only reason I achieved my goal was that I refused to give up—though I must admit that many times I felt like it. Now I can see the tremendous progress I made, but it was difficult to see at the time. Something inside me kept urging me on. I knew that I always wanted to be a professional classical ballet dancer, and I just wouldn't quit. I knew that it was part of the plan of my life.

What can you learn from experiences such as these? That no matter what obstacles you face in your life, it is important to keep on trying until you reach your goals. Sometimes an experience will lead you in a different direction than you had anticipated, but you have to be flexible. You also have to learn to do all that you can and then trust in the Lord to help you. I was not a member of The Church of Jesus Christ of Latter-day Saints during those years when I was studying ballet and trying to join a professional company, but I am grateful that the Lord heard my prayers and was there to help me when I asked. Sometimes answers to our prayers come in ways that we may not expect, but He does love us, and He is concerned about our well-being and happiness.

Years ago two young women, Debbie and Lisa, came to my home. Both had the same goal: to become Miss USA. Each was trying to improve herself. They both had the same problem with their figures: all the sand was in the bottom of their hourglass. I gave them each the same information and help. We figured out the colors and style of clothes that looked best on each, and I gave them the same exercise routine and diet. Then they returned to their homes to the same hectic schedules as they prepared for their pageant appearances.

A few months later, when I went to the Miss USA pageant, Lisa walked in and I couldn't believe what I saw. She had faithfully used the exercise routine I had given her and she looked fabulous! In fact, she won the swimsuit competition that year.

Then in "rolled" Debbie. Does that tell you how she looked? She had not only gained weight—she had gained a lot of weight. When she saw me, she started making all kinds of excuses. "Well, it was Thanksgiving, and you know how Thanksgiving is. I went home and my mom made me eat all this food. Then it was Christmas. You know Christmas! People bring all these goodies, cookies everywhere. I couldn't stand it." She went on and on through every holiday.

I thought to myself, these two young women each had the same goal. They had the same exercise routine and the same diet program. One of them followed her plan, and the other didn't. One paid the price, and the other didn't.

That's what I'm telling you about any type of goal you set for yourself. It will not be handed to you on a platter. It's up to you. You can be given lots of valuable advice on how to improve your life, but unless you do it yourself, it will not happen.

In life there are no easy ways to achieve success, no magic formulas you can follow or secret charms you can buy that will help you earn your goals. There is only one way. You must pay the price that can lead to you to goals you would like to accomplish.

CHAPTER
SIX

# CHOOSE HAPPINESS

Life is hard. When we came to this earth, we knew that we would face many problems. But we agreed to come because we also knew that our Heavenly Father wants us to be happy, and part of our happiness comes through overcoming and rising above our problems. He has told us, "Man is that he might have joy." Our greatest joys can come when we feel good about ourselves and know that we are doing our best to achieve our righteous goals, when we try to become all that we can become.

Because I speak at many firesides, youth conferences, and other large gatherings of young people, I often receive letters from youths who have heard me speak and who need help. In their letters they pour out their feelings about themselves and their circumstances. One young woman wrote to me:

*Dear Barbara,*

*You said if I ever needed your help in any way to just ask. Well, now I need your help. I need your advice desperately. My life is a mess. I have tried to work my problems out, but nothing is working. I feel like just throwing up my hands and giving up on life.*

*Recently our family moved to a different city. That's the whole problem. No one likes me, and I find myself alone constantly. While others are in groups all over school, laughing and having a good time, I am all alone wishing I were back home. I would give everything I have to anyone who would include me, laugh with me, be a friend to me, and honestly love me.*

*Nothing makes me happy anymore, but then why should I be happy if no one appreciates it? People just hate me. And it's* not *because I'm ugly, because I'm not. I'm chubby though. My mom says I'm not, but how can you trust your mom?*

*One of the things I like about myself the most is my artwork. I'm going to put one or two of my drawings in this letter. I think they're pretty good. But I guess other people don't like them, because they only glance at them and say, "Oh, that's nice." Don't you hate it when people do that?*

*Please give me your honest opinion on my drawing and please give me some advice.*

*Your friend,*
*Amy*

What would you say to this girl? Her feelings are real, and they are similar to those of many others I meet. This is what I wrote to her. Perhaps it will help you with your own problems:

*Dear Amy,*

*Your drawing is excellent. I minored in art at the University of Arizona, so I've been exposed to enough art to know when something is good. You definitely have been given a gift from Heavenly Father, but it will be up to you to take the gift and make it better. I have known many people who have gifts or talents but they take those gifts or talents for granted and never do anything with them. My advice to you is to keep working on yours. It can give you real happiness to know that you have done the best you can with the gift Heavenly Father has given you.*

Then, addressing Amy's problem of moving, of not having friends, and of not feeling happy and accepted, I told her the following story—not a true story, but a kind of fairy tale.

Once upon a time there was a family who had to move to a new city. When they arrived at the entrance to the new city, they were met by a gatekeeper. The family stopped to talk to the gatekeeper. They asked him, "Just what kind of city is this?"

The gatekeeper answered by asking, "What kind of town did you live in before?"

The family said, "It was awful. We had terrible neighbors. Our children went to an awful school where nobody smiled and nobody wanted to be their friends. Everyone hated them. We were all miserable because nobody appreciated us, so we decided to move."

"Well," said the gatekeeper, "I'm sorry to tell you this, but this is the same kind of town, with the same kind of schools and the same kind of people that you left." And so the family drove away.

Next in line was another family who had moved to this city. They asked the gatekeeper the same question: "What kind of town is this?"

And the gatekeeper answered the same way, "What kind of town did you live in before?"

The family said, "Oh, it was a wonderful town, full of wonderful people. Our children went to a great school where everyone was always happy and smiling. They had lots of friends and we hated to leave, but because of our father's job, we had to relocate."

The gatekeeper said, "Welcome to our town. It's just like the one you left behind."

In life you have many choices. You can choose happiness or you can choose sadness. The circumstances of your life, where you live, where you work or go to school aren't important, because it is what is inside of you that will come out. If you give love, you will get love back. If you're always smiling, people will smile back. If you want to feel comfortable in a new situation, it's up to you to make the difference.

The more you are a friend to others, the more they will want to be your friend. Make an effort to get involved in activities, and always offer to help people in every way you can. Then you will develop into a person who is liked everywhere she goes! It doesn't matter where you live or where you go to school. You can bring happiness and friendship with you wherever you are.

If you feel shy, you can do as Sharlene Wells Hawkes, who was Miss America in 1985, suggests: "Fake it until you make it." Pretend that you're not shy. Pretend that you're happy. Pretend that you enjoy keeping a smile on your face, and it will get easier and easier.

To help you through those downer times, here's a saying you can post where you can see it every day: "After the storm comes the rainbow." Then make another sign and put it right next to the first one. The second sign should say, "And this too shall pass."

No situation or set of circumstances is ever permanent. If you can just hold on, I promise you that things will get better. You have your bishop, your teachers, and your leaders that you can go to when you need help. They want to be your friends.

I also promise you that one day the painful problems you are facing now will be only entries in your journal. That may sound simple, but I know it is true. In my life I too have lived through many problems and setbacks, as you will read in this book. As I look back on those problems now, I realize that that is what they are: only pages in my journal. The terrible feelings and emotions are gone. Don't give in to your feelings. Cling to the truths you are taught. Later, when you look back on this time of your life, you'll be glad you didn't miss any of the exciting, happy, spiritual moments that can be yours. Give yourself time.

Most important, remember that your Heavenly Father loves you, and He wants to help you. Quit dwelling on your own problems and dwell on His love for you. Reach out to someone who needs your help, for it is in giving that we receive.

It's not easy at first, but ask Heavenly Father to help you. He is always there, and I promise that He will help you, for He has said: "Trust in the Lord with all thine heart; and lean not unto thine own understanding. In all thy ways acknowledge him, and he shall direct thy paths." (Proverbs 3:5-6.)

CHAPTER SEVEN

# TRUST IN GOD

After working on your own abilities and doing everything you can possibly do to help yourself, there is one additional step: Allow the one person who knows what is best for all of us to enter in.

When you have done your best, let God do the rest. Trust Him to guide your life as He wishes for your best good.

When you get ready for the basketball tryouts; when you are standing up to give your debate speech; when you are lined up to run a race at the track meet; when you're about to begin your college entrance exams; when you enter a beauty pageant; when you are standing to speak to a group with your stomach in knots, pause for a moment and say, "Heavenly Father, I have done all I can do. I am prepared. I consecrate my performance unto you." Then let go and let God. Trust in Him. And even if you don't take first in the competition or win the race, you can have His comforting Spirit and know that you tried. You can open yourself to feeling His love and concern for you.

I remember one particular day when this concept—let go and let God—helped someone unexpectedly. A reporter from the *San Francisco Chronicle* had been assigned to come to my house to interview me and Miss California, whom I was coaching, for a story on beauty queens. When he arrived, I could tell that he thought his assignment was a waste of time.

As I greeted him at the door, he said, "Do you know where I've been all morning? I've been interviewing the Pope."

I said, "That's wonderful." I could sense that he was saying to himself, "What a letdown. Now I have to come out here to interview this lady with this beauty queen."

He sat behind me as I began explaining the winning formula to Miss California. After explaining the formula step by step, using the same chart as you'll find in chapter 1 of this book, I said, "Diana, after you have done all you can, then you have to let go and let God. You have to trust your Heavenly Father. When you walk out on that stage, you have done all you can do. Now you have to let go and let Him decide what happens next."

I turned around and looked at the reporter, and he had tears streaming down his cheeks. A little concerned, I asked, "Are you all right?"

He said, "You know, I've been struggling with a really big problem in my life. I just realized something. I've done all that I can, and now I have to trust God with the outcome."

Well, he stayed all day. His story was featured on two pages in the newspaper, and on one of the pages was the headline "Let Go and Let God."

One other thing happened that day. I opened the Book of Mormon and read this scripture: "But behold, I say unto you that ye must pray always, and not faint; that ye must not perform any thing unto the Lord save in the first place ye shall pray unto the Father in the name of Christ, that he will consecrate thy performance unto thee that thy performance may be for the welfare of thy soul." (2 Nephi 32:9.)

I realized that this is what I had been telling all these young women. After disciplining yourself mentally, physically, spiritually, and socially, you have to take the next step, the one that leads to true success and happiness. You have to then turn yourself over to God's care and keeping.

As I look back on my life, I realize that I am where I am today because of a unique set of experiences that have not been easy. But one big truth I have learned from my life I can describe best like this: Life is like having two channels on a television set. Channel one is the way of the world. Turning to it is a way of saying, "My will be done." Channel two is the way of God and Christ. It is like saying, "Thy will be done."

We have the choice of which channel to tune in to. In my life, I have taken both routes. My childhood years ended at about age eighteen, when I went away to New York City. From then until I was about thirty, my life was on channel one. It revolved around Barbara. I was going to be a dancer, and that was the most important thing in my life. I went to New York and I failed—or thought I had failed.

When I came home, I was planning to marry a young man I had dated in high school. But everything blew up, and we didn't get married. I figured I had failed again.

My boyfriend's best friend liked me a lot, and we started dating. I wasn't really in love with him, but at that time all my friends were married, so when he asked me to marry him, I accepted him. I thought I had failed as a dancer, so what was left?

Well, my marriage was a disaster. I won't go into all the details, but I soon discovered that my husband was a manic-depressive: high one minute, totally depressed and destructive the next. And the thing he seemed to want to destroy most was *me.* We had a beautiful son, but that didn't seem to make things better between my husband and me.

Finally I wanted out. As I think back on this period of my life, I realize I was saying, "I want *my* way. My way is the only way." One night I sat in my living room, completely self-centered and tuned to channel one, and said to myself, "I don't care who I have to pray to, but I want out of this mess."

I had never heard of Joseph Smith in my life, but I can tell you that I felt the powers of darkness in that room when I made that statement. I know that Satan was there. I think he must have said something like, "Fine, now I'll open all the doors to you because you don't care who you pray to." The doors were flung open. My husband and I separated.

I went to Atlanta and signed a professional contract, but the company I was with went bankrupt. Then I went to Canada to another dance company. During that time, because I was feeling depressed, I was also taking pills a doctor had prescribed for me. I didn't know what they were, but they turned out to be amphetamines—uppers. When the prescription ran out, I crashed. I felt worse than I had ever felt in my life.

Since I had nowhere else to turn, when I returned from Canada I decided to go back to my husband. We tried to reconcile and had another baby, a daughter. I thought another child would help. But by then my husband was drinking heavily, smoking marijuana, and taking other drugs. He was totally out of control, and he finally committed suicide.

As I tried to pick up the pieces of my shattered life, I realized that the philosophy of channel one, "My will be done," was a disaster. It was time for me to change channels to the one that taught, "Not my will, but Thy will be done."

I moved to Dallas, where I was a single parent and ran a modeling school. Though I hadn't been to church for a long time, I decided to start going and to do the things I had been taught there and by my parents.

I remember going to church one day and reading this verse from the Psalms: "Thou wilt show me the path of life: in thy presence is fulness of joy; at thy right hand there are pleasures for evermore" (Psalm 16:11), and I remember praying, "Heavenly Father, I just want your will in my life. I have made a mess of things so far. Please show me the 'path of life' that you want me to take, so that I might know the 'joy' that comes from knowing you." That verse became my daily prayer. I was now in the "Thy will be done" channel.

The years as a single parent were difficult, but I later moved to San Francisco and eventually married Hal, who is my husband now. I continued going to church every day, studied the Bible, and even joined a Bible study group.

One summer, as Hal and I were winding up our vacation, we stopped in Salt Lake City for a couple of days. He was then going back to work in San Francisco, and I was going to go to El Paso to visit my father. After settling in our hotel, we went out for a walk. We walked toward Temple Square and saw an enormous building.

Hal said, "That's the Mormon temple. Would you like to go in and see it?"

I was shocked, "What, me – a Catholic – go into the Mormon temple?"

"It's no big deal," he said. "Just look at it as a historic landmark."

When we found out we could not go into the temple itself, we went into the Visitors Center to watch one of the filmstrips. Suddenly on the screen I saw a picture of Jesus Christ with His arms opened, and it was as if He were saying clearly, just to me, "Here I am, Barbara. Come follow me." And I *knew!* This was where I was supposed to be. I was converted right there on the spot.

It took the rest of my family a little longer. We went through ten sets of missionaries, but three years later, on December 12, 1981, our whole family was baptized together.

One last hurdle for me was coming to know without a doubt that The Church of Jesus Christ of Latter-day Saints is the true church. I had been raised a Catholic and had even lived in a convent for a year in New York City. It was very hard for me to wholeheartedly accept that there could be just one true church.

While I was struggling with this problem, I was asked to speak at a youth conference at Missouri State College. The speakers arrived a day early, on Thursday, for a leadership meeting, and we were up late that night helping the leaders make final preparations for the conference.

Friday morning the young people arrived. We had a full schedule of workshops and activities that day, followed by a dance in the evening. Afterwards several of the young women visited with me in my room until three in the morning. By the end of the conference, I was exhausted.

When the conference ended, the stake president invited the speakers to tour some of the Church history sites in Missouri. I was so tired that even the thought of such a drive was discouraging, but I decided I might never get an opportunity like that again. Among the sites we were going to visit were Liberty Jail, Far West, and Adam-ondi-Ahman. I said to myself, "Well, at least I know what Liberty Jail was, but I've never heard of those other places."

I kept falling asleep during the drive. We made some stops, then drove for a long time out into the country, and all I could think of was how tired I was. Then we arrived at a beautiful place called Adam-ondi-Ahman. We parked the car and started walking around. I broke away from the group, thinking that at least my son, John, would know about this place. I could pick a flower to press in my scriptures for him.

I walked down the hill and bent down to pick a flower. As I stood up, a cloud moved over a large tree nearby. In my mind's eye I thought I saw Christ. He was standing there preaching to a huge crowd—thousands and thousands of people.

I got down on my knees, tears were streaming down my cheeks, and whispered over and over again, "Jesus, I want to be here with you. I don't know why, but I want to be here with you." As I said these words, I felt that maybe I *could* be there with Him.

When we got back in the car and I had regained my composure, I asked my companion, "Has anyone ever said anything about Christ being here?"

"Get the book *The Millennial Messiah* by Bruce R.

McConkie," one of the men, a teacher of Church history, said. "It will tell you about Adam-ondi-Ahman."

As soon as I got a chance, I went to an LDS bookstore and found a copy of *The Millennial Messiah.* I was so excited that I sat on the floor right there in the bookstore and opened that big book to the chapter entitled "Adam-ondi-Ahman." In it I read every detail about what I had seen: Jesus would come to Adam-ondi-Ahman, and He would preach there to tens of thousands of people. It was all written exactly as I had seen it. I knew then, beyond a shadow of a doubt, that this was the one true church. The Lord had given me the answer that I needed and wanted.

I know that the Lord will give you answers for your own life. Make yourself available so that He can talk to you. Pray to Him. He is ready and waiting to help you.

## POPULARITY, LOVE, AND MARRIAGE

*Two subjects that cause a lot of unhappiness for young women are popularity and dating. Almost every girl wishes she could be the person everyone says hi to and talks to, the one who gets dates easily and finds "Mr. Right" without difficulty. I've asked Sharlene Wells Hawkes to tell you about some of her experiences with these problems:*

When I was in junior high and high school, I wasn't all that different from any other student. Everyone wants to be popular and accepted—so did I.

I ran for an office once in sixth grade, hoping to make it into the popular group, and didn't even make the final ballot. In fact, I got about five votes. I was so discouraged that I decided then and there I was never going to run for anything again. Ever.

The next year we moved, and I told myself, "Here's my chance to start over!" I was a new seventh grader, a new Beehive, and in a new ward. I was devastated when the girls who had grown up together refused to accept me. They left me out of everything.

Six months later we moved again, this time to South America. There in Argentina I attended an American school with my sisters, and again I found myself as the new kid on the block, with the distinct advantage that no one knew I hadn't been popular in the States. But I already knew from past experience that I wasn't the popular type of person, so why bother trying.

I didn't make too many close friends at first, and started living in the library between classes and at lunch. I also spent a lot of time at home practicing the piano.

But then something major happened. Toward the end of my eighth-grade year, one of my teachers told me that student-body elections would be coming up soon. In our school, there were four main student-body officers, one from each class. Since we were just entering ninth grade, my class had to present candidates for one of the offices for the next year.

My teacher told me that she thought I ought to run. I laughed. *Right!* I thought. I patiently explained to her that in order to win an election, you had to know a lot of people and they had to know you. In other words: you had to be "popular," which I most definitely was not. I continued on with a list of other things I lacked.

The school was pretty small, and families moved in and out frequently as their fathers were reassigned with the embassy, the military, or private businesses. So when my teacher asked me to name all the popular people in my class, I realized that *hey*—every one of them would be moving by the next year!

My mind all of a sudden went about ninety miles an hour. *What a chance!* I thought. With a void of popular people, someone like me might have a shot at it, right? I decided to try. I would run for office.

My family helped me come up with some cute posters (like "Oil wells? Water wells? No! *Sharlene* Wells!"), and I overcame my terror as I stood in front of the entire high school to give my one-minute campaign speech. I even started smiling in the halls and saying hi.

Well, I won the election, but I discovered that it wasn't winning the office that helped me make friends. I never did feel completely "popular" in high school, but I felt a lot better about myself. I found that when I smiled, people smiled back. When I was the first to break the ice and talk with them, even though I'm basically shy, they would talk back.

It all starts with you. If you're happy, then people want to be around you. If you're always complaining, who wants to be around that?

My effort to change didn't always go completely smoothly, though. When I was in ninth grade, I tried out for cheerleader. There were six openings, and about that many of us tried out, so I made it. About two months later I quit because of comments from some basketball players. They said I looked like a skeleton, and every time I did a cheer, they made fun of me. I knew they were just teasing, but I started to see myself as they saw me, and quit. I certainly didn't want the rest of the world to see me like that.

Cheerleading wasn't that important to me, but my singing was. When my economics teacher implied that I didn't have much talent, I just wouldn't accept that. Where my singing was concerned, I simply refused to quit. It was very important to me, so I kept working at it.

When I competed in the Miss America pageant, I sang and played the Paraguayan harp for the talent segment. After I won the title, I sang all over the country. With something as important to me as singing, I had to persevere even when the comments of others were discouraging. It's okay to take advice from other people, but you need to weigh it all. I had to realize that they were criticizing my voice, not me as a person. I had to take their comments with a grain of salt, learn from my experience, and keep trying.

Here's a list I've come up with, of five steps to being "popular":

1. *Take a risk.* Dale Murphy, the baseball player, said that even when he was in a slump, he would go to practice and swing hard. He always kept swinging hard, just in case

he hit the ball. What this means is: Keep trying. If I had kept my promise to myself to never run for office again after I lost the election in sixth grade, my life would have been very different. You just have to keep trying. Winston Churchill gave a speech once that consisted of nine words: "Never give up. *Never give up.* NEVER GIVE UP!"

2. *Avoid comparison.* Sure, it's easy to spend all your time looking at everyone else and thinking how much better they seem to be. When I was in the Miss America pageant, we were often lined up in alphabetical order, which put me next to Miss Texas, who was gorgeous. I remember once a crowd of photographers coming our way. Then one of them said to me, "Excuse me, Miss Utah, but could you please move over to one side? We need to take a picture of Miss Texas." I felt about two inches tall. But I couldn't let that bother me or make me feel insecure. I had to be happy and confident with who I was.

3. *Have a sense of humor.* When I was in high school, people would often make fun of me because I couldn't date until I was sixteen. And they would make fun of my friends and me for not drinking. We would joke about it, and people accepted it more easily when they knew that we could laugh about it but weren't going to give in.

4. *Stand up for what you believe in.* The world respects someone who is true to living righteously, even if you have to occasionally put up with some people making fun of you.

5. *Fake it until you make it.* Sometimes when you're in the middle of changing, it's hard to feel confident. If you have some good goals set for yourself and you know they're right, keep working toward them even if you feel like you're faking it at first. You'll gain confidence as you improve your skills.

When I was about thirteen, I received my patriarchal blessing, which said that if I lived worthily I would meet someone who would take me to the temple, where we would be sealed forever. Every time I looked at those words *he*

Sharlene Wells (Hawkes), Miss America 1985

and *him,* I thought, "There's someone waiting for me. But I have to live worthy of him."

Soon after that I remember putting together a list of what I thought "he" should be like. The first thing on my list was that he would be someone who put God before anyone or anything else—someone who respected his priesthood. My list went on to include a someone who was a returned missionary, who was responsible, and who was trustworthy. He also needed to be someone who loved his family.

My list was as long as I am tall. I had things on it like being athletic, since I'm athletic myself. I wanted someone with a sense of humor. I wanted someone who could go camping in the mountains, then come back the next day, put on a tuxedo, and handle himself gracefully in a social situation. I wanted someone with good manners, who knew how to be courteous.

At the bottom of my list was a little section I called "Optional." These were little things that weren't really important, but that would be kind of nice. That's where I put things like good-looking, having brown hair and brown eyes, etc. And I thought it'd be great if he were either a doctor or a rancher. At that time in my life, I was pretty much into the romantic "cowboy" image.

Through the years, I'd refer to my list a lot, but I just couldn't find anyone who fit *all* the requirements. I'd go out with someone thinking, *Oh, I'm just going out to have fun.* Then I'd get to liking him, and I'd start to think, *There is no way I'm going to find the man to match my list. Maybe I should just compromise.*

Fortunately, I allowed myself to be directed by the Lord and to listen to the promptings of the Spirit when I was told that one man or another was not right for me. If I had not let the Lord tell me what to do, I could have said, "I really like this guy. Maybe he doesn't fit my list, but hey—I like him and he can change." I'm sure glad I listened to the Lord!

When I met Bob, we were both juniors in college. We were in the same ward for a whole semester before we really noticed each other, and then at a ward social once, we started talking. I thought he already had a girlfriend, so I was carefree and open, because I didn't have to have my guard up or try to impress him. I remember thinking, *This guy is so honest. He would never do anything to hurt anyone on purpose.* He was responsible. I loved the kind of respect he showed me and other women. I remember thinking he was just a really terrific person.

Bob called me a week later and asked me out. For our first date, we planned to go see the lights on Temple Square at Christmastime. It was freezing outside, so he showed up in this huge red parka, looking like he was dressed for an Arctic dogsled excursion. And there I was, all dressed up in my mink coat! But he didn't seem flustered or apologetic, which totally impressed me. I loved how he just took it in stride.

For our second date, I asked him to come and help me

remodel our downstairs bathroom. I knew nothing about remodeling but was really excited to give it a try and do some interior decorating. It was also a kind of challenge—I wanted to see Bob being totally casual, and wanted him to see *me* being totally casual. I didn't have any makeup on and my hair was pulled back in a ponytail. Believe me, I did *not* look glamorous. We spent all day peeling wallpaper and painting, and had a great time.

During the course of the conversation that day, I couldn't help but mentally check off everything on my list. He's the youngest of ten kids and has strong family ties. He served a faithful mission. He is good to the core. He is *not* a flake. (I dated plenty of those, so trust me, I can tell the difference!) He's very athletic. He's also great-looking (of course, I'm a tad biased), and he's going to be a physical therapist. As for the ranching part, he grew up in a small one-stoplight town in Idaho, around dogsled teams and horses. We both are totally in love with the outdoors.

It was very important to me to find someone who would help me fulfill my patriarchal blessing, who would take me to the temple. I needed to find someone whom I could trust completely for the rest of eternity. I was falling in love really fast, and the great thing about it was that I knew that the Lord approved.

But one thing I knew even from age thirteen was that if I had a list of priorities for my future husband, he would surely have one for his future wife. I knew I needed to live so that I would be worthy of the person on my list—I needed to have the same qualities that I was looking for in a husband. Now that I'm married and I realize how important these qualities really are, and see the eternal happiness they can bring, I wouldn't trade them for all the popularity in the world.

## A Happy Ending

*I, Barbara, had the privilege of going to the Salt Lake Temple with Sharlene and Bob when they were married on July 5, 1987.*

*Sharlene looked as beautiful as an angel, and Bob looked very handsome.*

*Sharlene's father, Elder Robert E. Wells of the First Quorum of the Seventy, sealed them for time and all eternity. He talked to them about commitment, sacrifice, and love. Then he said, "I am so proud of you two. You have kept yourselves worthy. Your lives will be blessed."*

*After the ceremony, as we were leaving the sealing room, I went over to Sharlene and hugged her. Then she looked at me with the most beautiful and radiant smile and said, "Barbara, please give all the young women that you speak to a message from me. Tell them that winning the title of Miss America was absolutely nothing compared to going to the temple with Bob."*

*Later, I thought about what she had said. I thought, We can't all be Miss America, but we all can go to the temple. We know the things we must do to be worthy. The rest is up to us.*

OUTER
BEAUTY

CHAPTER NINE

## MAKING THE MOST OF YOUR OUTER SELF

We have talked a lot about inner beauty being the most important kind of beauty. It absolutely is.

But we do have an obligation to take care of ourselves and make the most of the temples of our spirits, our bodies. We can learn about good grooming, about taking care of our skin, about applying a little makeup artfully, about making good choices in what we wear. Feeling good about how we look can give us confidence to let our inner beauty shine.

Sharlene Hawkes has shared with me some of her feelings about outer beauty. This is what she said:

"Sometimes we condition ourselves into believing that we are just what we are. If we weren't born beautiful, forget it. We can't do anything about it. Wake up!

"If you had been with me when I participated in the Miss America pageant, a showplace for beautiful girls, you might have been shocked. When we were rehearsing our group numbers with no makeup on and hair straight out of the shower, we looked like a few softball teams getting together. You never would have guessed that you were looking at contestants for Miss America. Then when all the girls fixed themselves up, when we curled our hair and did what we could with what we had, it was an amazing transformation.

"What's on the outside doesn't count for more than 15 percent of the total score—and that's in a beauty pageant. So why should it count for more when you are taking a look at yourself in the mirror? What matters, obviously, is what's on the inside. Take the time to comb your hair and style it a little. Take the time to add a little bit—and I'm talking about a *little* bit—of color to your eyes, your cheeks, and your lips. When you feel good about yourself, your inner beauty all comes out in your smile. And that's the start of outer beauty."

Each of the Miss USA winners I've worked with has a beauty secret, something that has helped her to feel and look her best under pressure. These are their secrets, which they have agreed to let me share with you.

*Laura Martinez-Herring, Miss USA 1985:* "I believe in being an early riser and starting my day with prayer and meditation. It is also important to me that I eat the proper foods and practice good nutrition."

*Christy Fichtner, Miss USA 1986:* "Even if your hair is a mess and your makeup is melting and your clothes are wrinkled, keep a smile on your face. And always clean your face well before you go to bed, no matter how tired you are."

*Michelle Royer, Miss USA 1987:* "My most important secret is exercise. It not only helps a woman have a better figure, but it also improves her disposition and really helps her to deal with stress."

*Courtney Gibbs, Miss USA 1988:* "I can go without a lot of other things, but sleep is my most valuable beauty secret. Without it, the sparkle in my eyes is gone. I need at least seven hours of sleep a night—preferably eight."

*Gretchen Polhemus, Miss USA 1989:* "My best beauty secret is to drink lots of water—at least ten glasses a day, and nothing else. I don't drink diet soda or anything carbonated. I never starve myself, but I eat small portions of chicken, fish, fruits, vegetables, and whole-grain breads."

In this section you will find tips on colors to wear, how

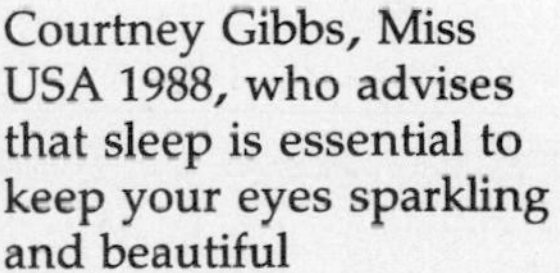

Courtney Gibbs, Miss USA 1988, who advises that sleep is essential to keep your eyes sparkling and beautiful

to find a "fashion personality" you feel comfortable with, organizing your wardrobe, makeup, hair, diet, and exercise. These are things I have learned as I have worked with beauty-pageant contestants as well as many other teenagers and women through the years. When you feel good physically and in your outward appearance, you will also feel better about your inner self and will have greater confidence and self-esteem.

## Your Best Colors

Over the past few years we've heard a lot about "having your colors done." One reason this type of consultation has enjoyed such popularity is because there is a lot of truth in the notion that certain colors look best on certain people. You really can benefit by learning about color and which colors look best on you. But it is not all cut-and-dried. Problems arise when things like this happen: You get some advice on what colors you should wear, so you go home and tell your dad, "Oh, I'm a winter person. My clothes are the wrong color. I have to throw everything out."

You do not have to throw out your wardrobe. You can correct problems with less flattering colors by using scarves, blouses, or jewelry in more flattering colors next to your face. You can be creative and find ways of making the things in your wardrobe work.

Sharlene told me that she had to learn the hard way that color is important. This is what she said: "I used to think all colors looked the same on me. I thought it just happened to be how I felt or what kind of mood I was in on a particular day that determined whether or not I looked good in them. But now, of course, I recognize that certain blues and certain reds, for example, enhance my features more than others. When I combine those flattering colors with my own style, I can make good wardrobe decisions."

It is important to learn what colors make you feel good and also look good on you. Knowing the colors of your skin tone can help you select the right makeup to use. Knowing about color will help you have more confidence in your choices.

Basically, there are two main classifications of color: warm and cool. The warm colors have a slight undertone of yellow, and the cool colors have an undertone of blue.

You have probably heard of the seasonal color theory, which recommends that summers and winters wear cool colors, and springs and autumns wear warm colors. For most people the seasonal theory works fine, but a small percentage of people do not fit neatly into one "season."

Everyone can wear some shade of each the primary colors (red, yellow, and blue), depending on whether the shade is warm or cool. For example, a warm-undertoned person can wear an orange-red, and a cool-undertoned person can wear a bluish red. Although green is not a primary color, everyone can also wear some shade of green. A person whose skin tones are warm can wear a color like chartreuse, and a person whose tones are cool can wear bluish green or forest green.

And you can usually wear the exact color of your hair or of your eyes. A dark brunette looks good in dark brown, the same shade as her hair, even though she may not be able to wear other shades of brown as easily.

You probably already recognize some of the colors that you look good in. If every time you wear pink you receive compliments, you might suspect that you look better wearing pastels than darker, more intense shades.

However, if you just don't know what colors look good on you, there are books in the library that will help you understand color, cool and warm undertones, and how to select your most flattering colors. Many cosmetic and clothing departments in department stores now offer this as a free service.

## Your Fashion Personality

If you want to develop good fashion sense and make wise clothing purchases, it helps to learn about your fashion personality. You have probably heard warnings about not indulging in every fad that comes along. If you analyze the types of clothes that look good on you and that you really like, you will be less inclined to make unwise impulse purchases.

Sharlene says that after she won the Miss America pageant, she was given some money to buy clothes for her public appearances. She had no idea what to buy. She said she thought that if a dress cost a lot, it must look good. She also let salesclerks talk her into buying some items. Now, looking back on it, she says that she was probably the worst-dressed Miss America ever. She hadn't figured out what she felt the most comfortable in and what looked best on her.

I agreed to help Sharlene sort out her problem in selecting her wardrobe. She got a wonderful job as a reporter for a television sports network, ESPN, and needed to look good on screen. But she was a newlywed, just out of college, and had little money to spend on clothes.

The first thing I had Sharlene do was to get a manila folder and start a collection of pictures. This is the first step in learning about your fashion personality. Thumb through fashion magazines and other publications, and every time you see a picture of an outfit you like, regardless of the cost, tear the page out or make a copy of it and put it in a folder.

Sharlene had great fun putting her dream wardrobe into a manila folder. Then, when we looked through it together, we saw a thread of sameness going through all the things she chose. Everything she picked out was either sporty or simply elegant. She didn't choose anything that was frilly. When she found out that her fashion personality fit into the sporty category, she said she finally understood why she had never felt good in one particular romantic dress in her closet.

Try this exercise for yourself and see if you can recognize your style. Don't worry if you don't fit neatly into one particular category. You can lap over into two or more, but there will be one major fashion personality category in which you will feel most comfortable. But if you can discover the type of fashion you like, then you can more easily avoid being swayed into unwise purchases by fads or by friends trying to talk you into things that really aren't you.

Following are descriptions of six basic fashion personalities.

1. DRAMATIC

People who have this type of personality are thought to be confident, self-assured, bold, exotic, and flamboyant. If this describes you, you are probably a dramatic. You want to stand out. You want to be unique and original. You dress with a flair.

*Personality:* You refuse to look like everyone else. You may be soft spoken or highly flamboyant. Either way, you're always noticed. In your environment, you either prefer a clean look (all white) or you have so much clutter that you've raised it to an art form. You love using odd things as accessories.

*Makeup:* You like to try new techniques in private and go out in public when your makeup is perfect.

*Hair:* You enjoy new styles, especially those that sweep away from the face.

*Clothes:* The style of a dress is more important to you than the material it is made of. You study trends and then make them your own. You do not follow fads, but if the style is right for you, you keep it long after others have quit wearing it.

*Fabric and Textures:* You tend to like sophisticated combinations and are not afraid to mix textures that don't seem to go with each other.

*Patterns:* You are attracted to bold and dramatic florals and strong geometrics.

*Accessories:* You like accessories that are dramatic. They tend to be large in scale and to make a statement.

2. SPORTY.

The All-American girl fits the sporty category. Sharlene discovered that this is her fashion personality. Her energy and up-and-at-'em attitude are typical of this type. Sporty people are natural and unpretentious. They tend to accept people at face value.

*Personality:* You have a spirited, "let's do it" approach to life. You want your clothes to be able to keep up with you. Comfort is very important, and you dislike that starchy, ironed look.

*Makeup:* You prefer a very natural look.

*Hair:* You always have washed, clean hair. You don't like to fuss over it. You prefer swingy, bouncy, blunt cuts. You dislike lots of spray and curling.

*Clothes:* You prefer styles that are tailored and conservative. You love to wear pants; straight skirts are too confining and full skirts are too cumbersome. You choose cotton instead of silk, solids instead of prints, khaki instead of white.

*Fabrics and Textures:* You like fabrics that are flat and smooth, such as wool. You also like suedes and leather.

*Patterns:* You like plaids, small checks, stripes, and small florals.

*Accessories:* Classic is the word. Jewelry must be plain and worn sparingly. You like natural things like wood or copper.

3. CLASSIC

People of this personality type have their lives pulled together. They enjoy having everything under control and like to think things through before trying them. The classic fashion personality is respected for her good taste.

*Personality:* You analyze what you have to do to accomplish something, then draw on your inner discipline to make it happen. Some people may be intimidated by your competitiveness. Because you are so organized, you appear calm. People think you don't ever worry.

*Makeup:* You take great care with your makeup, and it is never overdone.

*Hair:* Your hair is always clean and neatly shaped. You like to wear it medium length and are not eager for a change.

*Clothes:* You enjoy expensive-looking clothes in elegant styles. You find a hem length and stick to it (usually just below the knee).

*Fabrics and Textures:* You like smooth textures that are not too bulky or soft. And you never wear anything that is clinging or revealing.

*Patterns:* You prefer solids to prints.

*Accessories:* You go for understated elegance, with just the right chain or strand of pearls.

4. NATURAL

People of the natural type have a scrubbed, shining,

"real" look. They are usually small or slender—not fragile, but not large in any proportion.

*Personality:* If you are a natural, you are perky, bubbly, and friendly. You feel young at heart.

*Makeup:* You usually wear very little or no makeup, but sometimes you like to dress up with mascara, blush, and lipstick.

*Hair:* You like natural, casual styles, long or short. If you have curls, they are kept close to your face.

*Clothes:* You prefer a sportswear look. You like styles that are classic and tailored but definitely youthful. Your clothes are conservative and usually in neutral colors.

*Fabrics and Textures:* You prefer medium to lightweight fabrics that tailor well.

*Patterns:* You prefer small-scale checks, plaids, geometrics, and florals, and frequently wear solids.

*Accessories:* You wear few accessories, usually those that are small and natural looking.

5. ROMANTIC

The romantic type can be described in one word: soft. She enjoys a soft look and has soft manners and a soft heart. She is charmingly feminine, graceful, and sophisticated. Her lifestyle is "homemade," and her room has a slightly lived-in look.

*Personality:* Men enjoy you because you make them feel masculine. You like to wear pastels and soft fabrics. You will choose skirts over pants because they are more feminine. Everything about you is soft and friendly.

*Makeup:* You use grays and pastels for a soft, smoky look. Your look is natural, with no harsh liners.

*Hair:* You prefer softly curled, feminine styles.

*Clothes:* You like to combine high style and sophisticated lines with soft femininity. Your clothing is never severe. You choose sashes over crisp belts, pearls over gold, pale blue over electric blue, a flower to a pin, a ribbon to a chain. You would never wear a really short skirt.

*Fabrics and Textures:* You like rich, soft fabrics that have a lustrous feel and can be draped and tailored into soft lines.

*Patterns*: Typical patterns for you are plain or soft, with thin stripes, blended geometrics and plaids, and lacelike designs. You also like to wear plains.

*Accessories:* You like accessories that are medium in size and dainty in detail. For jewelry, you select small pearl earrings or precious stones.

6. ARTY

The arty fashion personality is a free spirit. She is her own kind of woman and not competitive with others.

*Personality:* You are a private person, on your own time clock. You're not a compulsive shopper. Your home is a crazy quilt of textures, crammed with unique mementos of your life. You don't often buy things that are new and shiny.

*Makeup:* You use either no makeup or lots of it. Your eyes are the focal point. You experiment with a dramatic look.

*Hair:* You enjoy dramatic hairstyles—long and frizzy or very short or streaked.

*Clothes:* Your clothes have to be individual. They often won't cost a lot, but they have to be interesting. You never buy an outfit featured in a store window. You aim for chic combinations, making your own mix and match with layers. You take pride in not spending a lot of money on clothes.

*Fabrics and Textures:* You enjoy wearing rough tweeds, nubby cottons, and antique lace.

*Patterns:* You feel comfortable in daring mixtures of patterns, such as pinstripes with antique brocade.

*Accessories:* You accessorize your outfits with large, pouchy leather or suede bags, hammered silver and brass jewelry, and antique pieces of jewelry.

Again, don't worry if you don't fit exactly into one of these categories. You can be a mixture, but one will be more dominant. But it is helpful to know how to recognize your fashion personality, so that you will not waste money buying things that other people talk you into, or that you feel pressured to get. When you can identify your own preferences, you will be more satisfied with your wardrobe.

## Organizing Your Closet

Now I'm going to give you an assignment, one that you may not like: Go into your room and take everything out of your closet.

Now put in a pile all those clothes you have not worn for two years or more—you know, those things that are too small or out of style or that you don't feel comfortable wearing. Pack them in a box and give them to a younger sister or take them to a charity, such as Deseret Industries or Goodwill.

Now examine the things that are left and make sure they are washed, ironed, and mended. Then hang them in your closet in order. Hang your pants together, blouses together, skirts together, and your dresses together.

Now look carefully at your shoes. Sort out those that need repairs—new heels, sewing, and so on. Take them to a shoe repair shop and have them repaired and cleaned up. Polish all the rest of your shoes, and put them back in the closet neatly and in order.

Next, think about the clothes remaining in your closet. How many outfits can you make out of them? It's more than you think. With mixing and matching you can make many outfits out of a few. Get a piece of paper and begin listing all the possible combinations you can think of: the green sweater with the black skirt; the green sweater with the white pants; the blue blazer with the plaid skirt; and so on. Include variations for each item of clothing. Then put the list in your closet or a dresser drawer where you can find it easily and can use it to plan what to wear. Then, when you wear a particular outfit or combination, make a notation on your list. Can you imagine how much more organized your life is going to be? You're going to have days of never wearing the same outfit because mixing and matching will expand your possibilities. You're going to be totally organized.

To ensure that the plan really works, however, you're going to have to do one thing more: Hang up your clothes when you take them off! Look each item over for dirt or spots and put those that need cleaning or laundering in a neat pile or hamper. Put those that need to be repaired in another pile. Plan time periodically to take care of repairs, so you can really make your list of possible outfits and combinations work for you.

If you do all this, you will look more "put together." You will look as if you care about yourself, and your wardrobe will look good. And there are some side benefits. When you organize one area of your life, you'll start to organize others. You're going to feel better about a lot of things!

## Skin-deep Beauty

You've heard the saying a thousand times: "Beauty is only skin deep." But the fact is, taking good care of your skin is one of the best habits you can have in taking care of yourself.

As I got into the modeling business, I decided that I was going to have my own line of cosmetics. It was while doing the buying for my cosmetic label that I became disenchanted with makeup. I flew to New York City and went to a major supplier to buy the things I needed. I walked into a huge warehouse. There were enormous sections just of eye shadows, and others of mascaras. At that time, I could buy eyeshadow for twenty-five cents apiece. I was told that I should mark it up five times. That's when I found out that all we really pay for when we buy cosmetics in a variety or department store is the advertising and the packaging. Many of the big cosmetics companies buy from the same sources and apply their own brand names on the packages.

Mascara is mascara; eye shadow is eye shadow; lipstick is lipstick. If you want to waste your money on expensive brands, go ahead. But they are all basically the same—only the packaging is different.

The only really crucial beauty product is a good moisturizer. As we get older our skin becomes dry and needs to be moisturized. Even oily skin needs a good moisturizer. Does a moisturizer put moisture in your skin? No. It protects your skin. That is why you should use a moisturizer every day.

Not every lotion or cream is designed to work as a moisturizer. First, the label has to say that it is a moisturizer. Read the label so you can avoid moisturizers that have as the main ingredient petroleum products or mineral oil.

One thing I have noticed is that as women get older, they get wrinkles, and often they put on more makeup to cover the wrinkles. The problem with doing that is that the makeup usually gets caught in the wrinkles and cakes there.

As women get older, they need to use less makeup, not more. If you use a foundation, be sure it is very sheer, or light. If you don't want to wear foundation at all, that's fine too. The trend currently is for a very fresh, natural, unmade-up look. But makeup does look nice, especially for special occasions.

Here are a few hints on applying makeup.

1. *Apply your foundation.* Use a sponge. You can buy all kinds of little makeup sponges that are inexpensive and of good quality. Dampen the sponge slightly, dot it with foundation, and apply it to your face evenly. Make sure your foundation is sheer and matches your skin tone exactly.

2. *Brush your eyebrows.* The days of plucked eyebrows are gone. Use an old toothbrush and brush your eyebrows up. Use a little mousse or hairspray on your brush to hold them in place.

3. *Apply eye shadow.* I got this hint from Sharlene: Make sure that the darkest color goes toward the outer edges so

that your eyes look larger. Go easy on the shadow—use just a hint of color.

4. *Apply eyeliner.* Use an eyeliner pencil rather than liquid eyeliner, for a more natural look. With the pencil, make tiny dots along your lashes. Then blend the dots together. You want the whole look to be very smoky and natural.

5. *Apply blush.* Follow the ridge of your cheek bones, and make sure the color of blush you use picks up your underlying skin tone. For example, use a peach shade rather than pink if your skin tone is warm. You shouldn't be able to see the outline of where the blush is on your cheeks. It should blend in and look natural.

6. *Apply lipstick.* Use a lip pencil if your lipstick runs into the cracks around your lips. But be sure the pencil is the same color as your lipstick.

7. *Brush on translucent powder.* Translucent powder is a thin, light powder that doesn't change the color of your face. It sets your makeup. If you put foundation on without setting it with powder afterward, your foundation will dissolve right into your skin in an hour or two. Dust a light layer of powder over your makeup, including your lipstick, and it will last for hours.

## Caring for Your Hair

Clean, shiny, healthy-looking hair is an important indicator of both your general health and how you feel about your personal appearance. Here are some tips for hair care:

1. If you shampoo daily, use a mild shampoo and change brands often.

2. Use hair conditioner sparingly. Too much conditioner can leave your hair limp and difficult to curl.

3. Have your hair, especially the split ends, trimmed every three or four months to keep it bouncy.

4. Brushing stimulates the scalp.

5. Remember that your hair is dead; the only living part

is *under* the scalp. Hair products can only coat the shaft, so watch out for false promises in advertising.

6. Don't overdo it with a blow dryer, hot rollers, or curling iron. Use these things sparingly and carefully.

7. If you have blonde hair that has a green tinge after too much chlorine during the summer, try rinsing it with club soda.

How you style your hair can make a big difference in your appearance. Don't wear the most "popular" style for this season if it doesn't enhance your features and the shape of your face. To find out your face shape, stand in front of a mirror and use a bar of soap to trace an outline of your face onto the mirror. Now stand back and study it. Are your facial contours oval, elongated, angular, or round? (See illustrations, page 82.) Here are some suggestions for possible hair styles for each of these shapes.

1. *Oval:* If your face is oval, you will have greater versatility in your hair styles because almost any style looks good on you. However, keep in mind the texture of your hair as well as your fashion personality. You can wear a side part or a center part, and either a long or a short style.

2. *Elongated:* If your face is in the shape of a long oval, a side part is usually best, with bangs if your forehead is high. To add width to your face, keep your hair full at the sides. Whatever you do, don't wear it long, straight, and parted in the middle.

If your face is more diamond-shaped, add width to the forehead by having your bangs fairly long. A side part works well. You also need fullness at the jaw line. A really full "bob" or page boy that is either chin-length or shoulder-length looks good.

3. *Angular:* If your face is square, wear a side part rather than a center part, and add height at the crown. Unbalanced lines will soften this face shape.

If your face is triangular, use fullness at the jaw line to give the illusion of width. Irregular lines are best, as is a side part.

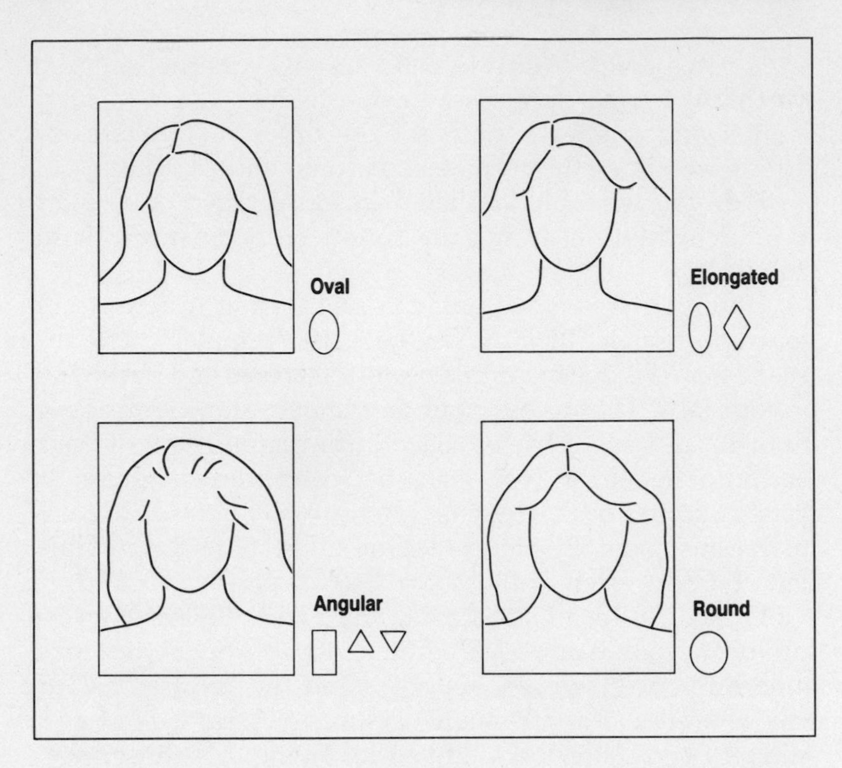


4. *Round:* With this shape face, use a side part and add some height at the crown. Whatever you do, don't have short curls the same length all over your head. Irregular lines look best. Shoulder-length works well.

A good, basic rule is that wherever your face is wide, your hair should be close to the head; wherever your face is narrow, your hair should go out to compensate.

CHAPTER TEN

# DIET AND EXERCISE

Weight control seems to be a constant obsession with many girls and women. I'm going to tell you what I tell all the young women I work with who participate in beauty competitions.

I don't have an amazing pill to recommend that will cause all your pounds to drop off. No one does. And not every weight-control program that you might hear about is going to work for you. Every individual is different from everyone else, and what works for one person may not work for another. We all have different genetic backgrounds, body types, and physiological makeup. There is simply not one program that will work equally well for everyone. But there are some simple truths about diet and exercise, and perhaps the most important one is that reducing calories and increasing physical exercise will help nearly everyone lose weight and tone up.

## No Time to Exercise? Think Again!

Have you ever heard yourself say, "I don't have time to exercise?"

You don't have time *not* to exercise.

Do you need to exercise if you are already slim? Yes.

Why? Because it will make you feel better and give you more energy. And if you aren't slim, exercise combined with diet will do wonders for your figure.

How many days a week should you exercise? I believe you should try to do some form of exercise six days a week, if possible. Most important, you should make it a habit.

First you need to find an exercise program that works for you. My daughter tried running, but she had all the excuses. The first day she said, "I can't run today because it's too cold." The next day, "I can't run today because my Walkman is broken." Then the weather would change, and she'd say, "I can't run today because it's too hot." Excuses will never make you slim!

I have decided that running isn't the right kind of exercise for me. After many years of dancing, I found that my knees were weak. But I *could* walk on a treadmill at 4.7 miles an hour with a five-pound weight on each wrist. And I do this every single day while I watch the news on television.

One woman I talked with said, "Sister Jones, you told me to get out and run. The first day I got as far as the mailbox. The next day I got past the mailbox to the neighbor's house. I thought, *I can't do this. I'm too fat!* Then I made it past the mailbox and the next *two* houses. Each day I'd go a little farther."

Pretty soon this woman was running five miles a day. That's the way exercise works. You start out slowly and gradually build up until you can continue for thirty to forty-five minutes or even an hour if you have the time or the inclination. This woman went from a size 18 to a size 6—but she didn't do it overnight. She just started out doing what she could do.

My husband has a saying: "Do what you don't want to do—and get what you want to get." What he means is that everything is hard before it becomes easy.

Some people run or jog. Others speed walk, jump rope, ride a stationary bicycle, or work out on a trampoline. The important thing is to find an exercise that you can enjoy, one that will increase your heart rate and test your stamina, and then to do it regularly. Be sure it makes you huff and puff. One way to test how well you are doing is to try to sing. If you can do so, you need to push yourself just a little harder.

## You and Your Diet

In recent years many diet books have been published, all written by individuals who believe they have found the ideal diet plan. The authors have one thing in common: each advocates a particular diet plan that has worked for him or her. And that does not necessarily mean it will work for you or anyone else.

Whenever you diet, it is essential that you do so only with the approval and supervision of your doctor. Avoid fad diets or any diet that stresses eating only one kind of food, and don't use appetite suppressants or pills that claim to "melt fat away."

If I have one big secret to pass on to you, it is this: If you want to lose weight, you have to stick to your diet day after day, even when you eat out and are tempted by luscious—but fattening—things on the menu. It takes time to lose weight, so don't become discouraged when the scales don't change as quickly as you'd like!

When I counsel women who want to improve their figures and lose weight, I suggest first of all that they cut back on sugar, fats, and salt. When I told Christy Fichtner that, she said, "What else is there?"

Sharlene Hawkes told me, "I can't live without a chocolate chip cookie every day."

I replied, "That's too bad, but just try cutting out one sugary thing that you love."

Sharlene cut out Froot Loops. She used to eat Froot Loops every single day.

Christy stopped at my house on her way to Taiwan while she was Miss USA, and we went to a restaurant to eat. Do you know what she ordered? A tuna fish salad that was loaded with mayonnaise, cream of broccoli soup, and an enormous cinnamon roll covered with pecans and gooey glaze.

I said, "Christy, I can't believe you. How can you look like you look and eat all this stuff?"

Do you know what she actually ate? One bite of each of those things. If that were me and most people I know, we would have polished off everything. Some people are satisfied with just one bite, but most of us can't stop. We have to eat everything on our plates, so we have to be very careful about what we put on those plates.

I know how hard it is to diet. When I was in high school and I got so fat that I couldn't button my skirt, I'd say, "Okay, this is it. I'm going on a diet." So I would skip breakfast and lunch. When I got home after school, I'd be starving, so I'd eat an apple. For dinner, I'd eat only a salad. I would do that for three days and I would lose weight.

But then the weekend would come, and my friends would invite me to go to the movies. I'd say, "Okay, but I'm not eating anything."

They would say, "We'll go out for pizza afterwards."

"Okay, but I'm not eating anything."

What happened when I got to the pizza parlor? I'd be hungry enough to eat a whole pizza by myself. And the next day I'd step on the scales and discover I had gained back every ounce I had lost.

So start your diet by cutting out one fattening thing. Start with sugar. If Froot Loops are your passion, as they were for Sharlene, cut them out. You'll be amazed. Just cutting out one or more foods loaded with sugar will help you start losing weight.

Here is another helpful hint. Often when eating out, you'll just have a salad at a salad bar—but then you'll add a ladle of blue cheese dressing. Now your salad has as many calories and as much fat as the Big Mac your brother just ate. My suggestion is to take in your purse a little bottle of low-calorie salad dressing. Then when you're away from home, you don't need to eat fattening salad dressings. I do it. It saves lots of calories.

Once at the Lido, an elegant restaurant in Paris, I ordered a salad without any dressing. It came just as I ordered it, and I took my little bottle of dressing out of my purse and started pouring it all over my salad. Suddenly the waiter rushed over to my table and exclaimed, "Madame, don't use hand lotion on your salad!"

He breathed a sigh of relief when I told him I was just adding a low-calorie dressing.

Every diet should include foods from the basic food groups: fruits and vegetables, milk and dairy products, whole grains, and proteins. The secret to good dieting is to have well-rounded, balanced meals each day that include foods from these groups – but to select those things that are low in calories and in sugars and fats, but that are high in nutrition.

Many excellent lists of foods and their caloric and nutritional values are available in bookstores and health-food stores. Invest in one now, and study it carefully. Then when you eat out or prepare your meals at home, you can make wise selections that will help you feel good and give you energy – and that will also help you to lose weight. You may catch yourself wanting to add butter to the vegetables or sugar to the cereal and berries, but it is easier to resist when you know how many calories are in butter and sugar. Try to eat foods more simply, without butter, sauces, or other fattening ingredients. I have never yet seen an apple hanging on a tree covered with caramel coating. I have never dug a potato out of the ground and opened it up and found butter, sour cream, and bacon bits already inside. Experiment with herbs and seasonings, which are calorie-free, to perk up your vegetables.

I practice what I preach. I don't have to lose weight anymore, thank goodness, but I was a yo-yo dieter for many years. As a classical ballet dancer, if you gained more than five pounds, you were laid off. You couldn't dance the next week.

I had a tremendous appetite, so I would eat six tacos one night, then I would fast next day. The following day, I would eat a whole pizza, then starve the day after.

That's the way I was going through my life until I met my husband. He told me, "You have to eat three meals a day with me."

How could I do that? It was very difficult for me to learn to eat three nutritious meals a day, because I liked to eat junk foods and at odd hours. But once I started eating regularly and selecting foods with greater care, I found that I didn't have to diet anymore—the excess pounds came off and stayed off.

I'm not perfect, however. Sometimes when I go to a restaurant, instead of ordering a salad I order a huge Mexican dinner. When everything is gone, including the tortilla chips, my husband says, "Well, you really laid your ears back on that one!" I don't feel bad about it because such lapses are the exception to the rule, and I don't do that more than once a month.

If you were to eat pizza only a few times a year, it probably wouldn't hurt you. In fact, you should allow yourself a treat occasionally. But the big word here is *occasionally*. Go ahead and have cake on birthdays; just don't eat cake every week. Break the habit of having a treat every day.

When you're lonely or bored or sad or angry or upset for any other reason, don't head for the refrigerator to console yourself with food. Don't think of food as your friend. Look for something else to do that will make you feel better. Take a long bubble bath. Go for a long walk. Read a good book. Rent a movie you've been wanting to see (but forget the buttered popcorn).

One thing that helps is to prepare a list of things you enjoy doing—not things that you ought to do, but those that you honestly like to do. Then when you feel like eating out of boredom or loneliness, pull out your list and select an activity.

If you have a habit of eating while you study or watch television, find a substitute, such as a tall glass of water with lots of ice and a slice of lemon. If you must keep your hands busy while watching TV, try doing some needlework, such as knitting, crocheting, or embroidering. That will help keep your mind off food.

I know it's difficult to stick to a diet. But once you make up your mind to do it, once you start losing weight and developing better eating habits, I guarantee you'll find that it was worth the effort.

Then when you go out with your friends and they order pizza, you'll find yourself ordering a big salad and adding your own dressing from the bottle you carry around with you. How will you feel the next day? Great! That's the best way of all to diet successfully.

CHAPTER ELEVEN

# PREPARING FOR A SPECIAL OCCASION

There are certain times in your life when you want to look and feel absolutely the best. Perhaps you've been invited to a special prom, or are going to a wedding or other fancy party. Here are some ideas to help you get ready for that special occasion so you will feel and look your best.

Before the big day:

1. Decide what you're going to wear. If you need to buy a new dress or shoes, don't wait to shop until the weekend before. You'll be too pressured then, especially if you can't find what you want. Allow plenty of time to find what you are looking for. If you plan to wear new shoes, break them in for a few days first. Then you can dance all night and won't run the risk of getting blisters. If you plan to wear an outfit that is already in your closet, check it early and make sure it is clean and pressed. Polish your shoes, and take care of any repairs, if necessary.

2. Get your accessories in order. When a young woman is preparing to go to the Miss USA pageant, we have her assemble all of the accessories she'll need for each outfit, put them in a plastic bag, and tie them around the clothes hanger. Then everything will be all together. Select your accessories early and put them together so you can find them quickly the day of the big event.

3. Stock your purse. Include lipstick and other cosmetics you might need for touch-ups at the party, a comb or brush, mad money—and an extra pair of stockings or pantyhose.

4. Plan how you will wear your hair. The day of the prom is not the day to experiment with a new hairstyle. If your hair needs trimming, have this done one or two weeks in advance.

5. Practice putting your makeup on. Too often, if you wait to put your makeup on at the last minute, you'll tend to put on twice as much as you would any other time. Practice with your makeup a few days before the party, to be sure you won't look overly made up.

Now that these things are all taken care of, here are some things to do on the big day:

1. Start out the day with a good serving of fruit. This will help both your breath and your teeth. If you eat pizza or a Big Mac on prom day, you'll have bad breath—and this is one day when you want to feel your very best.

2. Do thirty minutes of exercise that makes you huff and puff. Ride a bike, jump on a trampoline, jump rope, jog, or take a brisk walk. This will make you feel great and give you a healthy glow.

3. Steam your face: First wash your face well. Then fill a pot with water and bring it to a boil. Add chamomile flowers or rosemary leaves, if you have them. If not, plain water is okay. Turn off the heat and, being careful not to burn yourself with the water, drape a towel over your head to form a tent and let the steam go up all over your face for ten minutes, until your pores are fully open.

4. Once you have steamed open your pores, polish your face with just one of the following: granulated sugar, all-bran cereal, uncooked oatmeal, or ground almonds and honey. These are some of the things that top models and beauty queens use. An apricot scrub that you can purchase at a drug or department store will work also, but why spend the money when you probably have one of the other ingredients—which work just as well—in your own home?

First, put a thin coating of soap on your face and rub it in a circular motion. Now rub in the oatmeal or whatever you have chosen to use as a facial scrub, to remove dead skin. Then rinse your face well with warm water.

5. Put oil on your hair: Heat two tablespoons of pure vegetable oil or olive oil until it is warm. Then with your fingertips massage it into your dry scalp and through your hair. Wrap a length of ordinary kitchen plastic wrap around your hair and secure it well. Then forget it. You will need to keep the plastic wrap on your hair for a long time so it can condition your hair properly.

6. Remove the old polish from your nails. Then file them with an emery board the way you want them.

7. Next, prepare a mask for your face. For dry skin use one of the following: egg yolk, mashed avocado, or one teaspoon each of yogurt and honey. For oily skin, use one of these: egg white, rolled oats with warm water, or two tablespoons of honey with one tablespoon lemon juice and one tablespoon warm water. Spread the mask you select on your face—and then forget about it. Like the plastic wrap on your hair, it will be on for a long time.

8. Fill the bathtub with warm—not hot—water. Add one cup of milk (either powdered or regular) and a capful of one (please, just one!) of the following kinds of oil: corn oil, sunflower oil, vitamin E oil, or baby oil. While the tub is filling with water, put two big wads of cotton in a bowl of ice cubes. Then, with the plastic wrap still on your head and the mask still on your face, get into the tub. Put an icy wad of cotton on each eyelid, and settle back and relax for the next twenty minutes. As you soak, push the cuticles back around each nail.

9. If your tub has a shower, let the bath water out, then get under the shower. Remove the plastic wrap from your hair and shampoo thoroughly (it may take two or more washings to get all the oil out). Then rinse off the facial mask and the milk from your bathtub soak. If you don't have a shower, wash and rinse your hair, face, and body

with clear running water. If you use a conditioner on your hair at this point, use it sparingly; otherwise your hair will go "flat."

10. Shave your legs. Some women like to shave in the bathtub; some prefer to use a lotion. Do whichever you prefer.

11. Take time to clean the tub. All the beauty preparations you have used to this point leave a terrible ring.

12. Dry your hair.

13. Manicure your fingernails. I recommend that you don't use acrylic to lengthen your nails. Nails can't breath under acrylic, so once you start using it, your nails won't grow back to normal for a long time.

For longtime nail care, here is something that I *do* recommend: Ask a pharmacist to give you a little bit of white iodine. Mix equal parts of white iodine and olive oil. Put a coat of clear polish on your nails. When the polish is dry, shake the iodine and olive oil mixture and rub a little into each nail. The iodine penetrates the nail and the olive oil softens the cuticle. Use the solution every day, and you'll have beautiful and healthy-looking nails.

14. Apply your makeup, but don't overdo it.

15. Style your hair.

16. Put your party clothes and accessories on, and check a mirror to be sure everything looks good.

Now you're ready for your big date. Because you have taken the time to prepare, you should have a wonderful time!

CHAPTER TWELVE

## MAKING THE CHANGE

Making changes, even good changes, is hard.

We've talked about a lot of things that can make a difference in your life. You may have even come up with some ideas of things you want to work on. But it is hard. If it were easy, you would have done it already.

Let me tell you a little story that illustrates how comfortable it is to stay where you are.

In a little village in Africa, people were dying at early ages. Scientists from around the world were called in. After extensive research, they located the cause of the problem. It seemed that when the villagers had made the adobe bricks that they used to build their homes, a certain type of insect had become imprisoned in the bricks. Long-term exposure to the toxins from this insect were causing the early deaths of the villagers. The scientists presented their findings, and the villagers were given three choices. They could tear down their huts and rebuild, using bricks treated with insecticides. They could abandon their village and build elsewhere. Or they could do nothing.

Guess what they voted to do?

Even though the last choice meant early death, it was too difficult for the people to commit to making the necessary changes. They voted to do nothing.

We are sometimes like those African villagers. We resist change. I would like to give you an assignment. Remember the winner's formula in chapter 1? Here are some specific things you can do to get started.

To start improving your mental abilities, watch the news or read a newspaper every day.

To start improving your physical stamina, get a jump rope and work up to jumping it thirty minutes each day.

To start improving your spiritual life, read your scriptures for a few minutes each day.

And to start improving your social life, write a thank-you note to someone every day for two weeks.

These assignments are just to get you started. As they become habit, add to them.

It's difficult to develop new habits, but just remember this little story my husband told me: One day a little boy wanted his father to take him fishing. The father didn't want to go, but he also didn't want to disappoint his son. The father dumped a complicated puzzle of the world on the glass table in the front room. He told his son that when he got the puzzle put together, they would go fishing. He thought it would take the boy several days to put the puzzle together, but just a few hours later, the son appeared and reported he had completed the puzzle. Amazed, the father went to look. Sure enough, the puzzle was complete. The father asked his son how he had worked the puzzle so quickly, and the son explained, "It was easy. On the other side was a picture of a man. When I put the man together, the whole world fell into place."

That is how it is with each of us. When we put ourselves together, then everything else will fall into place as well. Here is a letter I received a year after I talked with a young man. He made the effort to change.

*Dear Barbara Jones,*

*There really aren't words for what you've said and how you've changed everything for me.*

*Before I went to the youth conference I was seriously thinking about suicide. I was unpopular in school, ate lunch all alone, and was a little chunky. I also felt unloved.*

*Well, after meeting you, I decided to get rid of the sad, depressed me. I lost fifteen pounds, bought some cool-looking clothes, and got to know some new friends. They were a great help. They helped me gradually change myself.*

*Now the new me is active in school, and I have a leading role in a musical play. I feel as if a fifty-pound jacket had been lifted off my back. People who wouldn't look at me last year are now friendly. Even my parents trust me more now. They aren't worried about me, and they like my friends.*

I want to conclude with personal messages from some of the lovely beauty pageant winners with whom I have worked and whom I have come to love.

*Laura Martinez-Herring, Miss USA 1985:* "The real you is the best you. Just be yourself and have a really positive attitude. People will love being around you if you are a happy, positive, enthusiastic person. This is the way that I live my life, and I know it works. People like to be around those who are enthusiastic and who love life."

*Christy Fichtner (who became a member of The Church of Jesus Christ of Latter-day Saints in October 1985), Miss USA 1986:* "My message of counsel and advice is that you master the use of the winner's word NO. There are many temptations in the world, but if you can learn to say no to those temptations, then I promise you that your life will be blessed. The choices are yours. Listen to the promptings of the Spirit and then follow what you know to be right."

*Michelle Royer, Miss USA 1987:* "When God made you, He broke the mold. You are uniquely special. I spent twenty-two years trying to be someone that I wasn't, twenty-two years of comparing myself to others and trying to fit into their molds, before I learned that I didn't have to be like anyone else. There was no mold for Michelle Royer. I was the only one. And I thank God every day of my life for

Gretchen Polhemus, Miss USA 1989: "My beauty secret is to drink lots of water—at least ten glasses a day. I don't drink diet sodas or anything carbonated, and I eat only small portions of food."

helping me realize that I can just be myself and be content with who I am. I hope that you will come to that same realization."

*Courtney Gibbs, Miss USA 1988:* "I know God has a very special plan for my life, just as He has for yours. I just do my very best with the talents He has given me, and then I relax with the confidence that His plan is perfect for me. When I competed for the Miss USA title, I asked for a priesthood blessing from Sharlene Wells's father, Elder Robert E. Wells. I felt such peace and calmness during and after that blessing, and I know that God was directing me. His will for my life is all that I want. He has a perfect plan for your life too. Just do the very best you can each day, and then trust Him."

*Gretchen Polhemus, Miss USA 1989:* "I received a priesthood blessing the night of the Miss USA pageant, and I felt God's presence so strongly. When it was over, I said, 'If I win tonight, I am going to dedicate my entire year to the Savior, to do all things in His name.' I was totally relaxed knowing that the outcome was in His hands. The greatest advice I can give you is to live your life in service to others, just as the Savior did. That is where you will find your greatest happiness and inner peace. I know because that is where I found mine."

*Christina Faust (who became a member of the Church in December 1988), Miss California USA 1989:* "I was baptized on December 12, 1988, and it was the most incredible thing that has ever happened to me. I've become close to the Lord, and I know this is changing my whole life. Pay close attention to the things that Barbara has tried to teach you in this book. She knows what she's talking about. She's a truly great lady, and I love her with all my heart. Good luck to you. Believe in yourself, believe in God, and try to be the best you can every day."

To end this book, I want to finish my letter to Laurie, the girl who wrote me the letter that made this book happen:

*. . . and so, Laurie, I thank you for writing, and I thank all the other young people who have written to me. I am touched and honored that you would feel that the Lord sent me to you and to a lot of other girls. It is my sincere prayer that the things that I have shared with you in these pages will help in some small way to make your life better.*

*Your friend, Barbara*

*P.S. If I can help you—or anyone who reads this book—with a personal problem, please write to me in care of Deseret Book, Publishing Department, P.O. Box 30178, Salt Lake City, Utah 84130. I will write you back!*

May the Lord bless you!

# INDEX